PATRICK KAVANAGH
AND *THE LEADER*

PATRICK KAVANAGH
AND *THE LEADER*

THE POET, THE POLITICIAN AND THE LIBEL TRIAL

Pat Walsh

MERCIER PRESS
IRISH PUBLISHER – IRISH STORY

MERCIER PRESS

Cork

www.mercierpress.ie

Trade enquiries to CMD BookSource,
55a Spruce Avenue, Stillorgan Industrial Park,
Blackrock, County Dublin

ISBN: 978 1 85635 664 0

10 9 8 7 6 5 4 3 2 1

A CIP record for this title is available from the British Library

Printed and bound in the EU.

Contents

The Irish are a fair people – they never speak well of one another.

Samuel Johnson

Acknowledgements

I would like to thank Seán Kehoe, Fionnuala Carton, Phil Duggan, Mary McCaughan, Helen Power, Dympna Reilly, County Librarian Mairead Owens and the rest of the staff of Dún Laoghaire-Rathdown Public Libraries.

Evelyn Flanagan and Eugene Doyle of UCD Library Special Collections, Seamus Helferty of UCD Archives, Nuala Byrne of the Law Library, Sara Smyth and Jennifer Doyle of the National Photographic Archive, and Sandra McDermott and the rest of the staff of the National Library were the essence of helpfulness during my research.

Elinor Wiltshire and Declan Costello were very obliging when called upon, as were Adrienne Carolan and Stephen Rae of Independent Newspapers.

Thanks also to Mary Feehan, Wendy Logue, Patrick Crowley and the team at Mercier, and to Eoin Purcell for his support at the beginning of the project.

All quotations from the writings of Patrick Kavanagh are reprinted by kind permission of the Trustees of the Estate of the late Katherine B. Kavanagh, through the Jonathan Williams Literary Agency.

Patrick Kavanagh, Bloomsday 1954.
Courtesy of the National Library of Ireland

Introduction

'Yous have no merit, no merit at all'

He was not even in the country when the profile was published. Kavanagh had been staying in London with the family of an old friend from Ireland. He felt it prudent to leave Dublin for a while after the demise of his short-lived magazine *Kavanagh's Weekly* in July 1952. The journal that the offending profile appeared in was not one he would read even if he was in Dublin. *The Leader* had all the hallmarks of a tired publication, getting by with a small circulation, surviving on past glories, such as they were. But a friend from Ireland drew his attention to the profile.

He was horrified but not surprised. Ever since the collapse of *Kavanagh's Weekly*, Patrick and his brother Peter had awaited reaction from the establishment. The magazine had folded after thirteen frenetic weeks, but not before the brothers had vented their spleen with regard to all that was wrong with the Ireland of 1952. Week-in and week-out they had attacked Ireland's ruling class.

And now it had come. As Patrick saw it, the establishment was striking back. And he was not one to turn the other cheek. Patrick read its description of him:

... hunkering on a bar-stool, defining alcohol as the worst enemy of the imagination. The great voice, reminiscent of a load of gravel sliding down the side of a quarry, booms out, the starry-eyed young poets and painters surrounding him, all of them twenty or more years his junior, convinced (rightly, too) that the Left Bank was never like this, fervently cross themselves, there is a slackening, noticeable enough, in the setting-up of the balls of malt. With a malevolent insult which, naturally, is well received, the Master orders a further measure, and cocking an eye at the pub clock, downs the malt in a gulp which produces a fit of coughing that all but stops even the traffic outside. His acolytes, sylph-like redheads, dewy-eyed brunettes, two hard-faced intellectual blondes, three rangy university poets and several semi-bearded painters, flap.

'Yous have no merit, no merit at all', he insults them individually and collectively, they love it, he suddenly leaves to get lunch in the Bailey and have something to win on the second favourite. He'll be back.

Who had written it? A friend? An acquaintance? Patrick had his suspicions. In fact he had several suspects in mind. Of one thing he was sure, it had to be someone who was often in his company. The profile was close enough to the bone in its portrayal of him, remarking on 'his solid, peasant cunning ... the self-preserving instinct of the country-boy thrown among the rough crowd of city gurriers whose only thought is to do him down, to put something across him'.

And sure enough the writer of the profile had a view on *Kavanagh's Weekly*, with Patrick's brother Peter coming in for particular criticism:

... a typical product of the Irish free educational system, and one who, despite his travels among the grand seigneurs, has retained a basic GAA mentality, his brother had had a strong influence on Mr Kavanagh [Patrick] and it reached its peak-point with the collaboration on the *Weekly*. Like the ephemeral magazines that suppurate in schools and universities, it was designed to minister to the young editor's genius, and in the absence of other outlets for his literary efforts, to enable him to express his cogitations on the profundities of politics and economics without fear or favour. Few things, indeed, were favoured in it while it lasted, and it was obvious that the Irish nation was regarded with a particular amount of disfavour, though it was not clear whether this was not due to the fact that several of its most revered institutions, *The Irish Times*, the News Agency, the *Standard*, the Department of External Affairs, Radio Éireann, had either lost Mr Kavanagh's services or had refrained from calling upon them.

The profile went on, with heavy sarcasm:

Afraid of the magazine becoming a commercial success (though this seemed to imply an unwarranted lack of faith in his own integrity), and afraid, too, it may be assumed, of its revelations sweeping the Government from power and, with thousands of refugees streaming from the city, of being left with the country on his hands, Mr Kavanagh closed down after twelve issues. His brother, resplendent in a white bawneen jacket, green pants and a yellow tie, departed for America, there to denounce, not Hollywood films, not spivvy ties, not American manners, not the American way of life, but the harmless little gatherings of Irish exiles in the United States. One cannot be other than touched and amazed at the strength of the umbilical cords that bind both Mr Kavanagh and his brother to Mucker.

The profile went on to pay tribute to Kavanagh as the author of 'The Great Hunger', 'the best poem written in Ireland since Goldsmith gave us "The Deserted Village"'. Patrick saw this praise as mere lip-service because the article then proceeded to describe the controversy over certain sections of the poem, which resulted in him being visited by the police and threatened with imprisonment. It detailed how the Department of External Affairs had refused to pay Kavanagh's passage to the United States to enable him to deliver a series of lectures. This was envisaged as part of a scheme for the development of cultural relations between Ireland and other countries.

Having left its praise to the end, Kavanagh doubted its sincerity – 'Left-handed compliments' as he described it at a later date. Patrick could not let it lie. Although he believed that Peter had strong grounds to sue, he decided that, as the elder and more famous brother, it was his job to uphold the honour of the family by taking action. He contacted his solicitor. At the very least he would extract an apology and a retraction. Not only that, there was the possibility of substantial damages and he could do with the money. He also didn't believe *The Leader* would allow the case to go to court.

Chapter 1

'Poetry is a luxury trade'

In 1904 Patrick Kavanagh was born in the townland of Mucker in the parish of Inniskeen, a rural area of County Monaghan, roughly half-way between Carrickmacross and Dundalk, not far from Hackballscross. Kavanagh was one of nine children. Having left school at thirteen, he worked as a cobbler, his father's occupation, and on the family farm. For twenty years he lived life as a small farmer, toiling for his father in the fields, which as the eldest son he expected to inherit one day. There was little to distinguish him from his neighbours. He participated in the local social life, playing cards, going to dances, helping out on neighbours' farms. He even played football for the Inniskeen Gaelic football team. Goalkeeper was his position.

However, sometime during his teens Kavanagh developed an interest in poetry. He began writing poetry, submitting these poems to local and national newspapers, and gradually he improved. His earliest poems were printed in 1928 by the *Dundalk Democrat* and *Weekly Independent*. Three more were published by Æ (George Russell) in *The Irish Statesman* in the period 1929–30. Having come to the notice of Æ he was encouraged by him to persevere with his writing.

In those early years of his literary career, 'Patrick continued to plough and sow those watery hills of Shancoduff'.[1] Kavanagh always had an acute sense of place and throughout his life place names from his home area recurred in his work: Kednaminsha, Rocksavage, Drumlusty, all evocative local names. Like many an aspiring poet, it was a struggle to establish a reputation, but Kavanagh persevered. Eventually, a collection of his early work, *Ploughman and Other Poems*, was published by Macmillan in 1936. He saw recognition by an English publisher as a substantial step forward.

In 1938 Kavanagh moved to London in search of literary work. Impressed by his rural background Michael Joseph publishers suggested that he write a memoir of his Monaghan upbringing. *The Green Fool* was published later that year. He remained in London for about five months but could not settle there and so he returned to Mucker. However, finding himself more and more dissatisfied with life as a small farmer, he increasingly spent time away from Inniskeen and in 1939 he finally left to try and make a living in Dublin. According to his brother: 'Patrick's hope was to find some simple way of making a living … He felt that he deserved some sort of civilised position'.[2]

Later in life he claimed that this move was 'the worst mistake of my life. The Hitler war had started. I had my comfortable holding of watery hills beside the border. What was to bate it for a life? And yet I wasted what could have been my four glorious years, begging and scrambling around the streets of malignant Dublin.'[3]

Kavanagh was thirty-five years old when he left the farm for good to try and break into the literary circles in Dublin. Single and hungry for recognition, he arrived in Dublin, a naïve outsider, with little idea of how he was going to earn a living. Never the most diplomatic person and lacking a formal education, there were no obvious jobs for which he was qualified. He did not know it then, but he had little hope of acceptance into Dublin's elite literary circles.

Kavanagh had no regular income. His autobiography *The Green Fool* had hardly earned him anything. As his brother put it, his income was 'not enough money to keep himself in cigarettes'.[4] It was, at best, a hand-to-mouth existence, so it is little surprise that he came to see that 'poetry is a luxury trade and a man has no business adventuring into it unless he has buckets of money. In its truest manifestation, where it gives judgments, poetry is super-luxury. It would be interesting to see what would happen to a High Court judge if he were forced to follow the true poetic formula, doing the job for love, being forced into pubs for relief.'[5]

In the beginning of his time in Dublin, according to Anthony Cronin, Patrick enjoyed 'quite a prolonged honeymoon with literary Dublin'.[6] He was seen as some sort of peasant genius from the depths of rural Ireland, primitive and poetic, an image that he was later to regret. But as Cronin described it: 'He was enormous, uncouth, and, to a large extent, unlettered'.[7]

During his early days in Dublin Kavanagh was not a heavy drinker. He described Frank O'Connor, an early mentor of his, as a 'bun man', a man who preferred cafés and restaurants to pubs. In this sense Patrick too was a 'bun man' in his early years in Dublin. The type of woman he preferred was more likely to be found in the cafés on Grafton Street than the literary pubs in the area. Pubs were strongly male at the time and only the more bohemian and less genteel female ventured into those male bastions. However, unlike Frank O'Connor, who was a teetotaller, Kavanagh did drink and over time his consumption of alcohol was to become a problem. Although he claimed he hated drink, he became a heavy whiskey drinker over the years. It could be suggested that his lack of success drove him to use alcohol as a means of alleviating his pain and isolation and forgetting his poverty.

Kavanagh had no steady income and was constantly scratching around for whatever he could get via money-making schemes like smuggling farm produce across the border[8] and making poitín.[9] He held out hope that some influential patron like Archbishop McQuaid might find him a job. Kavanagh had originally met McQuaid when he had given a talk in Blackrock College. At that time McQuaid was President of the college. The archbishop occasionally gave the poet money, but what Kavanagh told him was that he really wanted permanent employment, although it was not so much a regular job as a regular income he desired. Kavanagh, in his somewhat obsequious and self-pitying correspondence with Archbishop McQuaid insisted that he had accepted handouts from him as though there was the prospect of a job at the end of it all.[10] He told McQuaid: 'I should have long ago gone to England. And yet ... I am not sorry I stayed ... All I will say is that there must have been special grace attached to your money. Believe me, Your Grace, I do not say this in flattery. Flattery, I abhor, for it insults my critical intelligence.'[11]

Kavanagh goes on to tell McQuaid that he was beginning to realise how hated he was: 'By whom I ask myself? And the answer seems to be the world.'[12]

Eventually Kavanagh was fixed up with a job with the *Standard*, a conservative Catholic weekly, edited by another Ulsterman, Peadar O'Curry.[13] However, *The Irish Times* with its pro-British views would have seemed a more obvious outlet for Kavanagh's journalism, as he could have been regarded as anti-nationalist by the political standards of the day. He did write for that paper but only on an occasional basis. Kavanagh had a poem called 'Spraying the Potatoes' published in *The Irish Times* in July 1940. Subsequently a number of letters appeared in the paper, poking none-too-subtle fun at the agricultural nature of the poem. Flann O'Brien and some of his UCD pals dragged out the controversy for as long as they could. As Kavanagh's biographer, Antoinette Quinn puts it: 'The underlying message was that Kavanagh was a country bumpkin, a complete outsider in Dublin and should not aspire to write for city newspapers'.[14] It is a curious irony that one of Kavanagh's poems indirectly led to O'Brien (Brian O'Nolan) being employed by *The Irish Times* to write his 'Cruiskeen Lawn' column.

An unlikely saviour for Kavanagh was English poet John Betjeman who was press attaché at the British embassy during the war. He is said to have offered Kavanagh a job as a spy for the British in Lisbon. It was proposed that he insinuate himself into Nazi circles by posing as an anti-British

Irish republican. It is hard to tell how genuine the offer was, but Kavanagh took it seriously enough. According to Peter Kavanagh, Patrick began to learn the language, taking a Hugo Course in Portuguese.[15] He later claimed: 'Only a technicality at the highest levels caused this to fall through.'[16] It is difficult to picture the outspoken Kavanagh, so conspicuous even in his own capital city, as a double agent in Lisbon.

Kavanagh was not long in Dublin when he turned vehemently against the Celtic Twilight school of literature. By attacking his peers in poetry and prose, he alienated possible employers, damaging his economic base and driving himself still further into poverty and isolation. Kavanagh did this all his life; moving on while destroying his bridges behind him. His disdain for his fellow poets was something he did not bother to conceal.

In a self-mocking article in *Envoy*, Kavanagh gave details of his time as a staff member at the very Catholic *Standard*: 'So eager was he to succeed as a sycophant in the pious line that he had nine names for the Pope – The Pope, Holy Father, His Holiness, Supreme Pontiff, Vicar of Christ, Visible Head of the Church, Angelic Shepherd, Successor of Saint Peter, Bishop of Rome ...'[17]

While he claimed to be a practising Catholic, he could be quite irreligious. On being told of the death of Cardinal McRory, he remarked: 'Now he knows what I always knew.'

'What's that then?' enquired the editor of the *Standard*.

'There's no God!'[18]

Northern poet and friend of Kavanagh's, Robert Greacen remarked upon the contradiction: 'Yet Kavanagh, in my presence, again and again emphasised his belief in God and in Mother Church, and his contempt for atheists and agnostics. He liked to shock, so the story about the bishop may be true.'[19]

On occasion Kavanagh called Greacen a 'Protestant bastard', which Greacen took to be an affectionate term, 'almost as if he envied my background. It was a signal that he liked me, for he had a ready stock of vulgar phrases to describe some impeccable Catholic bards who had incurred his wrath.'[20]

Anthony Cronin recalled Kavanagh telling him that the Catholic religion was 'a beautiful fairy story for children' and that 'it didn't do most people much damage because they didn't take it seriously, whatever they might think. Sensitive, imaginative people like himself took it seriously, however.'[21]

Prim and proper, middle-class Dublin looked down on Kavanagh. Even the literary sub-culture sneered at his rural background. On spying a man on a cart of manure passing by, Seumas O'Sullivan, Irish poet and editor of *Dublin* magazine was reported as saying: 'I see Paddy Kavanagh is moving; there go his furniture and effects.'[22]

Even a sympathetic observer like Michael MacLiammor remarked on his outsider nature: 'When some Dubliner, with more malice than wit, nicknamed Patrick "The Ploughboy about Town" it was generally accepted that the rustic aspect of the poet – those pendulous shaggy clothes, those lean arms interlocked athwart the chest, that battered hat crammed over the back of the skull ... that husky despairing voice, those lingering vowels ... was a deliberate adoption.'[23]

As Benedict Kiely, a fellow writer and northerner put it:

'He was a rough sort of man but he was touched by genius and by God'.[24]

Literary Dublin could be fearsome in its feuds and petty jealousies. Cyril Connolly, no stranger to backbiting, once retreated from the literary haunt that was the Palace Bar, declaring it 'as warm and friendly as an alligator tank'. He concluded that the bar was 'a cultural excrescence'.[25]

It was, perhaps an element of defensiveness that led Kavanagh to develop his notoriously abrasive public persona. As Robert Greacen put it: 'I doubt whether friendship came easily to Kavanagh. Life had taught him to be on his guard.'[26]

According to his brother: 'Those whom Patrick abused for their political, literary and other immoralities, were not slow in coming to their own defence. Their response was to pin on Patrick the label of outlandish poet. He was warned that financial success would ruin him as a poet, so too would a decent job and marriage. He needed, he was assured, the goad of poverty to continue writing his magnificent verses.'[27]

Peter claimed that this was Patrick's handicap to advancement, his 'immense, angular integrity'.[28]

Chapter 2

'All my own work and I got no training'

In September 1942, the *Irish Press*, the youngest and liveliest of the three large Dublin-based daily newspapers, hired Kavanagh to write a regular twice-weekly column. The newspaper was a well-known advocate of Fianna Fáil's and seemed an unlikely home for Kavanagh and his vehemently anti-de Valera views.

The column was intended as a 'City Commentary', the diary of a country person living in the capital, and in that context Kavanagh fitted the bill perfectly, having left his farm in Monaghan only three years previously. He picked the pen-name Piers Plowman to underline his rural background and indeed his literary credentials. In his first column he laid out his plans:

My object in writing these notes is to give a countryman's impression of city life for the benefit of my friends in the country. I want to reveal in a simple way the usual – and unusual – life of the city; the corporation workman, the busmen, policemen, the civil servants, the theatres, Moore Street and also, what occupies so large a place in Dublin's life, the literary and artistic.

> Do not get the idea that Dublin is not an integral part of
> Ireland, that spiritually, mentally and nationally, it is a thing
> apart. That would be completely untrue.[1]

It was a very wide brief and Kavanagh chose to write about whatever caught his fancy. As it was late September one of his first columns was on the All-Ireland Football Final, which as luck would have it featured Dublin. They were playing Galway and Patrick claimed to be a neutral observer, only deciding which team to support after the throw-in. Perhaps, for diplomatic reasons – though that seems unlikely – he opted to back Dublin. Most of his country cousins generally supported Dublin's opponents. It was a wet day and as he put it: 'the greasy ball was as hard to control as an eel on a shovel'.[2] Patrick had picked the winners. Dublin triumphed: the score was Dublin 1-10, Galway 1-8.

Sport became one of the mainstays of the 'City Commentary'; football, camogie and horse racing in particular. The weather, the passing seasons, were mentioned in lyrical terms in the early columns but less so as time went on.

As Benedict Kiely put it, Kavanagh treated his part of Dublin as if it was a rural town: 'Baggot Street, if you look at it, has all the characteristics of a street in a country town: it even has a bridge at the end of it, small shops, everything that Paddy needed to make him feel he was walking up and down Carrickmacross on a market day.'[3] Perhaps it was how he made the big city manageable.

Another early column featured a conversation with a shopgirl: 'Since the cigarette scarcity, I have developed friendships with girls in tobacconists' shops ...' He went on to give details of his chat with a particular young girl, who was lamenting the vicissitudes of her love-life. Patrick concluded: 'Anyway she gave me the twenty from under the counter.'

The war in Europe was referred to in a detached way, scarcity of food, drink, cigarettes and petrol being the most pressing matter. At one point Patrick reported that a chemist told him that he was getting a northern accent from all the Belfast girls coming into his shop looking for lipstick. Lipstick was rationed in Northern Ireland and so they travelled to the south to buy it.[4] The Emergency, as it was called in Ireland, left the country isolated from the continent.

Patrick's generally gregarious and inquisitive nature gave him sufficient material for his column. He did his serious writing early in the mornings and spent much of the working day on the prowl out on the streets of Dublin. He kept his eyes and ears open. He delighted in the turns of phrase of the ordinary citizens of the capital. In one column he describes a slow Saturday night after the pavement artist on O'Connell Street had gone home leaving his chalk pictures of Eamon de Valera, Jim Larkin and some movie stars to fade away slowly, '... another artist was re-making their outlines and later on I saw this lad waiting beside his cap, against which was the legend: "All my own work and I got no training".'[5]

This gentle, whimsical tone was characteristic of his columns. Patrick wrote about whatever attracted his attention: the work of a chimney sweep, an invasion of Argentine ants in his flat, two swans fighting on the canal near Lansdowne Road, going home for Christmas, a pawnbrokers' strike, boys fishing on the Liffey. He described ordinary scenes of city life, queuing for buses or attending the Feis Ceoil: 'In Henry Street a man was singing through a megaphone. The singing had the merit of being the worst I ever heard.'[6]

He showed a keen interest in camogie, though he was not always convinced of the sporting quality of the matches, describing one encounter as 'a killing-a-rat sort of game'. He recalled meeting four chatty camogie players from Queen's University Belfast on a train. They offered him a seat and struck up a conversation and Patrick was delighted with himself. He later wrote some doggerel in his column to commemorate yet another camogie match, one he described as being 'as lively as a stocking sale at Guiney's':

> Bright shone the sunlight on Peggy and Doreen,
> Wild swung the ash sticks. Be careful asthoreen!
> Josie is getting right into her stride now,
> Kathleen is hurling with all of her Cork pride now,
> A shout from the side-line: 'Mark your man, Kathleen Cody
> Kathleen pucks it, I tell you that puck was a dotie.
> The game is exciting, it is indeed really
> Maureen Cashman is tackling bold Ide O'Kiely ...[7]

Not one for the anthologies!

He was not beneath name-dropping in the column and described with pride casual meetings with widely known people he met on the streets. Most of these were inconsequential encounters but occasionally there was some substance to them: 'At a street corner I spent half an hour trying to convince Mrs Sheehy Skeffington that the presence of only two women deputies in the Dáil is no sign that women are inadequately represented. Women are an influence rather than direct rulers ... I think the majority of women hate being in a position of authority over men, it is contrary to nature.'[8]

John Betjeman, William Saroyan, Professor Julian Huxley, Margaret Burke Sheridan, Jack B. Yeats and Michael Scott were among the names Kavanagh dropped. He gave every impression of being remarkably contented with his life in Dublin at the time.

Kavanagh also publicised cultural events that he felt were worthy. Contrary to his image in later years, he was quite prepared to go to the ballet and opera, and donned formal suits to do so. He sat in on a lecture in the Institute for Advanced Studies in Merrion Square where: 'The "pupils" were mostly professors from the universities. There were a couple of priests, a Chinese and at least one attractive girl of whose face I caught a glimpse as I went out ... And so I go out into the cool air of common humanity once more. People are coming and going or standing chatting at corners, talking petty talk. Now for a nice cup of tea.'[9]

He showed his keenest eye for young women. He wrote of a particular waitress who was his favourite, or bantering with café staff to get extra sugar for his table.

Kavanagh used his column as a platform for his views but not to the same extent as in subsequent papers for which he wrote. The columns also provided very little evidence of Patrick's social conscience. They were formless and aimless, if amiable in tone, as he eavesdropped on conversations at bus queues or in cafés.

His writing continued when he was on holiday. The 'City Commentary' was re-titled 'Tourist Commentary' for the duration while he reported from Cork and Kerry in August 1943. He visited Dingle and Kruger Kavanagh brought him to meet Peig Sayers who by then was living on the mainland in Dunquin. Patrick was impressed by her, saying that she reminded him of literary women he had met elsewhere: 'Actually she resembles nothing as much as a woman writer. If she were holding her salon in Bloomsbury and not in a little cottage at the foot of the Kerry mountains one would not be surprised.'[10]

Most of the pieces were lightweight as Patrick was busy with his more serious creative writing. The columns give the impression that they were quickly thrown together, in a relaxed, easy-going, optimistic style. Nothing was too trivial for inclusion and this was perhaps its charm: 'As I was writing this I sneezed. Through my open window from a room across the alley, came the gay, bemused whimsical response of some strange girl – "God bless you". A thing like this cheers a man wonderfully.'

It is doubtful if the *Irish Press* got what they wanted with the 'City Commentary'. They were perhaps looking for a more rural angle to the writing that Patrick provided and in February 1944 they stopped the column.

Chapter 3

'I expected every poet to have a spare wife'

The Kavanagh family had always shown an amateur interest in the law. Back in Inniskeen, Patrick's father James, a shoemaker and farmer, had advised his neighbours on the making of wills, using a well-thumbed copy of *Pears' Encyclopedia* of 1891 as his textbook. He also gave advice on land disputes.

Patrick Kavanagh had a number of encounters with the law courts during his literary career. In 1939 Oliver St John Gogarty sued him for libel over a reference in *The Green Fool*. Gogarty was well-known in Dublin literary circles, perhaps most famous in later years for appearing in James Joyce's *Ulysses* as the character Buck Mulligan, an identification that he heartily disliked. Gogarty practised as a surgeon and throat specialist in Dublin. The relevant passage in *The Green Fool* referred to Kavanagh calling to Gogarty's house in Ely Place in Dublin and being greeted at the door by a woman in white: 'I mistook Gogarty's white-robed maid for his wife – or his mistress. I expected every poet to have a spare wife.'[1]

It seems to be an ironic joke aimed at Kavanagh's naïveté as much as anything else; the wide-eyed countryman with an inflated view of the glamorous life of the literary elite. However, this was not how Gogarty saw it. This innocuous enough remark, Gogarty claimed was defamatory, damaging to him in his vocation as a doctor in that it showed that he 'had flaunted immorality openly at his professional address'. Gogarty had himself been sued previously over a reference in his own memoir, *As I Was Going Down Sackville Street,* so he may have been in a litigious frame of mind. In *As I was Going Down Sackville Street* Gogarty had referred in disparaging terms to two Sinclair brothers who were antique dealers and art patrons. One of them had successfully sued and had won £900 plus costs. During the case Gogarty had denied that *As I Was Going Down Sackville Street* was 'somewhat Rabelaisian' and also that he had used quite a deal of poetic licence. The Sinclairs were Jewish, which laid Gogarty open to the accusation of anti-Semitism. The loss had so embittered Gogarty that he had quit his practice in Dublin and moved to England.[2]

Gogarty's biographer, J.B. Lyons, was of the opinion that the case against Kavanagh was taken out of a desire 'to take a bumptious upstart down a peg'.[3] The printers and publishers of *The Green Fool* were sued in the English courts and the case was heard in March 1939. Kavanagh was not called as a witness. Appearing for the defendants, Mr G. Slade asked Gogarty: 'Do you agree that poets are entitled to a certain amount of licence?'

Gogarty replied: 'Poetic licence.'

Gogarty accepted that 'green' as used in the title *The Green Fool* could be taken to mean that the author was 'young' or 'inexperienced' and naïve in what he wrote.[4] In his closing statements the defence counsel argued that just because something was 'offensive and in bad taste did not make a statement defamatory'. However, the jury found in Gogarty's favour and he was awarded £100 damages plus costs.[5] The finding against *The Green Fool* was a substantial setback for the publishers Michael Joseph, and cannot have helped their relationship with Kavanagh. The book was withdrawn from circulation.

Years later, according to John Ryan, Gogarty was reported as having claimed that 'what really hurt him about the passage was not so much the slight to his wife, but the suggestion that he had only *one* mistress'.[6] To further complicate the matter, Kavanagh had made it all up. The incident had never taken place. He could not, however, use that as a defence in a libel case.

The loss of the case seriously damaged Kavanagh's confidence: 'Ay – *The Green Fool* business,' he later told a journalist, 'the libel action over the head of it – did me a lot of damage. It destroyed the momentum.'[7]

Yet Patrick's memory of this libel action may have led him to believe that libel actions were a guaranteed source of money. In a letter to Peter dated 15 October 1952, Patrick, who was visiting London at the time, wrote: 'By the way, the Dublin paper, *The Leader* run by Brian Inglis has written a fierce profile on me with abusive references to you, which is a nasty libel on me, and I am planning action from here ... there may be money in it ...'[8]

As Irish author Honor Tracy put it: 'Libel actions are especially plentiful, which need amaze no one. The libel laws of Ireland ... are an open invitation to truffle hunters at any time ...'[9]

Kavanagh himself had taken an action against the British and Irish Steampacket Company in 1940. He had been knocked off his bicycle in his early days in Dublin by a horse-drawn lorry owned by the company. In evidence Kavanagh stated that at the Tara Street junction with Butt Bridge he had waited to receive a signal from the traffic policeman. Having received the signal he had proceeded a few yards when the shaft of the lorry struck him from behind causing him to fall. He claimed that the bicycle was completely wrecked and that he wasn't able to do any work for about six weeks. He stated that he wrote novels and verse and did special work for newspapers, such as an article on the climbing of Croagh Patrick on Reek Sunday, which had appeared in that *Irish Independent* that very day.

'Were you at Croagh Patrick?' asked Judge Shannon.

'Yes.'

'I liked it [the article] very much.'

'Thank you very much, my lord.'

In further evidence Kavanagh claimed that he never counted what he made from his writings but he supposed it would average £5 a week. He had agreed to give a broadcast talk for Radio Éireann the day following the accident, but he had not been able to do so. Not only that, his clothes had been damaged and his nerves were badly shaken for a long time.

The British and Irish Steampacket Company denied

negligence and pleaded contributory negligence by Kavanagh. However, Kavanagh was awarded £35 and 3 shillings, a substantial amount in 1940.[10]

The hat, the glasses, the large hand holding a cigarette. John Ryan, editor of Envoy *was also a gifted cartoonist, catching the essence of Kavanagh's public image.*

Chapter 4

'The sacred keeper of his sacred conscience'

The relationship between the Kavanagh brothers intrigued Robert Greacen: 'Peter's ideas and opinions seemed almost identical with Patrick's ... He had the education, Paddy had the genius.'[1]

Greacen occasionally asked one of the pair: 'Where's your brother?' only to get the off-hand answer: 'How do I know?' as if to suggest that the bond between them was not strong. Yet his impression was that 'even if the brothers had a falling out from time to time – as seemed likely – each was highly defensive of the other'.[2]

And yet, Patrick could be ruthlessly competitive. Peter recounts a story from his early teens when he tried his hand at writing verse: 'When Patrick discovered what I was up to he told me I should give it up. The possibility, he said, of there being more than one poet in the same family was beyond belief and possibility. By poet he did not mean verse writer. The poet was unique ... since I had no desire to be another verse writer I took his advice.'[3] He wrote no more poetry. Whatever else might trouble him, Patrick never doubted his poetic ability.

Patrick was over ten years older than Peter though they had shared a room in Mucker. Peter had gone to a secondary school in Carrickmacross, the only one of the Kavanagh siblings to do so. In the years Patrick worked the farm and developed his interest in poetry, Peter shared his brother's dreams and hopes. In many ways Peter looked up to his older brother. Due in the main to the difference in their ages, Patrick took the lead with Peter acting as the junior partner.

When Patrick won a prize for his poetry in 1928, it was Peter who rushed up through the fields to Cassidy's where his brother was pitching sheaves at a threshing and gave him the good news that some of his poems were going to be published in a national newspaper. Patrick later described that moment: 'I have only felt excitement three times in regard to my work. The first of these was one morning when I was pulling the chaff from a mill at a threshing, my brother, who was a schoolboy at the time, came running up to bring me a letter from the *Weekly Independent* which when I opened it read, "the editor was accepting three poems" of mine …'[4]

Peter never lost that brotherly pride in Patrick's achievements. The relationship between them could be compared to that between Stanislaus and James Joyce, or even Theo and Vincent Van Gogh, the sensible brother giving support, financial and otherwise, to his more gifted, more wayward brother.

Peter carved out a career as an academic and a writer, publishing books on Irish theatre and Celtic mythology before devoting himself to maintaining his brother's reputation, becoming, as he saw it, 'the sacred keeper of his sacred conscience'.

They had some major falling-outs though as Patrick tended to treat his younger brother poorly, heedless of the pain he was causing. Money was often the root cause of his bad behaviour. The Kavanagh holdings consisted of three small fields and a bog around the house in Mucker and, half a mile away, the farm called Shancoduff, which had only been bought in 1926. In 1949, Patrick sold Shancoduff without telling his brother. As Peter put it: 'The farm was as much mine as his, the only difference being that his name had been put on the deeds by our parents'.[5]

Patrick got £450 for it and tried to soften the blow for Peter by telling him that he intended to invest the proceeds in buying a house in Dublin. He never did of course and soon the money was gone.

It is ironic that those few acres, which he wrote evocatively about for most of his literary life, did not remain long in his hands. If he was sentimental about the land and feeling any pangs of loss at selling it, he hid it well. In later life, he quoted approvingly a Monaghan neighbour who told him, 'Kavanagh, do you know what it is, you're the only bloody man that ever made money off that farm',[6] although it was not with the shovel but with the pen.

Peter Kavanagh made an estimate of Patrick's income in his early years in Dublin. It makes grim reading. However, these figures may underestimate Kavanagh's earnings because as Anthony Cronin delicately put it: 'There were always elements of concealment in his finances':[7]

1940

The Irish Times	£2.00
Irish Independent	£3.50
Law-Suit Award	£35.00
AE Memorial Award	£100.00

1941

The Irish Times	£6.50
Irish Independent	£1.25

1942

The Irish Times	£11.00
Irish Press	£49.00
Archbishop McQuaid	£5.00
The *Standard*	£9.00

1943

The Irish Times	£2.00
Irish Press	£148.00
The *Standard*	£13.00

1944

The Irish Times	£1.50
Irish Press	£5.00
The Bell	£5.00
Archbishop McQuaid	£5.00

1945

The Irish Times	£4.00
Irish Press	£1.00
The *Standard*	£8.00[8]

As Kavanagh himself explained, Dublin was a place 'where they thought so much of the poetry that they didn't believe in the poet eating'.[9]

'A POET IS NEVER ONE OF THE PEOPLE'

The brothers shared a flat on Pembroke Road. Their bachelor existence was stereotypically untidy, a byword for domestic squalor. As John Ryan, editor of *Envoy*, described it: 'The bath itself bore sad testimony to Patrick's wifeless existence, being full to the brim with empty sardine and soup tins'. The window had the rear view mirror from a truck attached to it so Patrick could observe callers at the front door without them knowing.[10]

Kavanagh's routine was to get up at dawn and write through the morning. He then spent the rest of his time out and about: 'He used to prowl round the streets like a hungry wolf and get especially restless before the evening papers appeared. Paddy … devoured news of all kinds – politics, racing, gossip. For him the world had dwindled into a parish not unlike his own native Inniskeen.'[11]

Kavanagh haunted the streets, 'newspapers under arm, eyes baleful behind horn-rimmed glasses, the enormous hands projecting behind each elbow, hat on head. Often as he walked he talked to himself or, scowling, muttered at the ground.'[12]

As J.P. Donleavy put it: 'This man, his powerful arms folding his big farmer's hands across his chest, walked the streets like a battleship plunging through the waves'.[13] John Ryan recalled: 'He liked talking, particularly to himself and quite loudly too ... brusquely and noisily ... a characteristic he had inherited from his father.'[14]

Kavanagh could be discourteous in public. 'Pedestrian encounters were quick and decisive ...' Donleavy gives a not untypical example: 'Have you got a pound to give me?'

'No.'

'Well, fuck off then.'[15]

He could be even more cutting in private. Kavanagh professed to despise phoniness. Donleavy described a characteristic response to a contribution to *Envoy*: 'Rubbish, utter drivel and the most appalling nonsense I ever had the disinterest to read.'[16]

He was convinced that an artist must be true to his life to be successful in his art. The painter, Patrick Swift, recalled that the first time he met Kavanagh he was told that he was 'nothing but a gurrier and a fucking intellectual fraud'. Kavanagh, on a later occasion relented somewhat and advised the young artist: 'You shouldn't be wasting your time with fucking phoneys ...'[17]

In the midst of such fearless judicial pronouncements it is little surprise he alienated much of literary Dublin, but Patrick was unapologetic. He answered to a higher calling: 'A poet is never one of the people. He is detached, remote, and the life of small-time dances and talk about football would not be for him. He might take part but could not belong.'[18]

He had no time for poets who exploited their Irishness: 'Strip their writings of this local colour and see what remains. Their outlook is similar to the sentimental patriotism which takes pride – or pretends to take pride – in the Irishness of a horse that has won the Grand National – with the emphasis on the beast's Irishness instead of on his horsiness.'[19]

He also disagreed with the promotion of the Irish language: 'The position is: the Gaelic language is no longer the native language; it is dead, yet food is being brought to the graveyard.'[20] This was one of the areas of disagreement that may have led to Kavanagh's notorious feud with Brendan Behan. Behan and Kavanagh had never really got on. According to Behan's biographer Ulick O'Connor: 'There was a rivalry between them which is not easy to understand between men of similar temperament who should have had interests in common'.[21]

As Anthony Cronin put it, Behan 'aroused in Kavanagh feelings of loathing and apprehension which are, on the mere face of it, difficult to explain'.[22]

Kavanagh was repelled by Behan's brash exhibitionism. There was an element of fear in it too. Behan, with drink taken, could become very abusive, not just verbally, but physically too. In one of the first references Kavanagh made about Behan, in a letter he wrote to Peter, he described him as 'a jailbird'. Behan spent time in prisons in England and in Ireland, mainly due to his activities in the republican cause. He had been caught with a bomb in England and had brandished a revolver and fired a shot at a policeman at a Bodenstown Wolfe Tone commemoration. From the age of sixteen to twenty-two, Behan spent all but six months of his life in confinement of some sort. Almost two years were spent in Hollesley Bay Borstal in Suffolk, and from May 1942 until July 1946 he was incarcerated in a succession of prisons in Ireland: Mountjoy Jail, Arbour Hill and the Curragh Camp.[23] The child of a socialist-republican family, Behan was an idealist, who had joined Fianna Éireann, the youth branch of the IRA, at the age of eight. He was also a fervent Gaeilgeóir and his earliest literary publications were in the Irish language.

Dublin being essentially a small town, Behan and Kavanagh could not avoid meeting each other. Cronin describes Kavanagh's reaction to Behan: his 'huge frame would become visibly agitated. The great shoulders would shake, the enormous hands fidget nervously, the long head swivel from side to side in search of allies or openings; and, unless well protected by company he trusted, the poet would frequently flee into the night.'[24]

Behan had a Dubliner's disdain for his country cousins:

> Those of the bogmen who could speak Irish I could exchange greetings with, but I could not understand the English-speakers very well … I speak Dublin, Belfast, Cockney, Geordie, rhyming slang, but like Nehru, I have no common tongue with the majority of my countrymen from the interior … whatever about the pen being mightier than the sword – it's lighter than the stockbrush.[25]

As Anthony Cronin put it: 'One of Brendan's special prides, amounting almost to an obsession, was the fact that he was a Dubliner. All those who had the taste to be born elsewhere were "culchies" … or bogmen … They were supposed to possess traits of character, particularly avarice and cunning, from which those born in the slums of Dublin were singularly free.'[26]

One can easily imagine how a palpable peasant like Kavanagh would antagonise Behan. A typical example of the mockery that Kavanagh could not abide is given by John Cooney, biographer of Archbishop McQuaid. In a public house Kavanagh accidentally dropped a letter from Archbishop McQuaid. Behan picked it up and read it. From then on to annoy the poet Behan would mime Kavanagh kissing the archbishop's ring.[27]

They were different in many ways: Behan was from the capital, Kavanagh was from the country; Behan loved the Irish language, Kavanagh did not; Behan was a physical-force republican, Kavanagh was not; and Behan was bisexual, which may have unsettled and repelled the more conservative Kavanagh.

Behan occasionally worked with his father's business as a house painter. If he spotted Kavanagh in the street below he would shout from the scaffolding. He habitually called him 'the fucker from Mucker'. Among the other names he had for him was 'Paddy the wanker', in reference to the controversial allusions to masturbation in Kavanagh's poem 'The Great Hunger'. It was one of those curious feuds where one of the participants took it much more seriously than the other. Behan seemed to unnerve Kavanagh, who saw something malevolent in him, something fiendish.

Unlike Behan, who seemed to embrace recognition and notoriety with gusto, Kavanagh was somewhat uncomfortable with fame. Patrick wanted renown as a poet and a man of letters, but at the same time: 'I hate praise, too – and publicity. A man wants to be alone. Publicity's a cancer. It eats out a man – till there's nothing but a shell left.'[28]

Kavanagh's large, clumsy peasant stature was much remarked upon. Larry Morrow wrote a profile in *The Bell* titled 'Meet Mr Kavanagh' using the pen-name 'The Bellman':

> … whether you like or dislike him, Mr Patrick Kavanagh, poet, novelist, autobiographer, film critic and (to some) Stage-Irishman about town, has become so fabulous as to be almost a figment of his own imagination … where Mr Kavanagh is concerned indifference is impossible … you either scream for him or against him … Even Mr Kavanagh himself is in a state of almost chronic hoarseness, screaming at himself, be it said, both for and against. And – let it also be said – he seems vastly to enjoy it, neither boastfully nor bashfully.
>
> There can hardly be a film-star's publicity agent who would not give a considerable 'cut' off his fees for the secret of the build-up with which, in a few short years, Mr Kavanagh has become surrounded … like all who wilt under the fierce beams of publicity, Mr Kavanagh, never runs to form – good, bad or indifferent.[29]

As proof of this unpredictability, Kavanagh arranged to meet Larry Morrow, not in a pub but in a fancy restaurant. 'The Bellman' describes the awkwardness of the big man in the dainty restaurant, always on the point of knocking something over: 'For Mr Kavanagh – both mentally and physically, as well as vocally is constructed on what the sculptors call the "heroic" scale, which is to say, rather larger than life.'[30]

The writer goes on to describe the poet's face as somewhat equine: 'There is too, more than a hint of a gargoyle about it.'

'I reserve the right to tell whatever lies come into my head', Kavanagh warns you in a stevedore's whisper, 'I've been telling lies all my life.'[31]

Larry Morrow was so impressed by the poet, he referred to Kavanagh in a different article as a 'thundering Irish one-man act'.[32]

As time went on, the public image that Kavanagh took on, took him over and he became almost a parody of himself; the rough, rude and crude countryman adrift in the big city. The mask became armour. Dubliners celebrated him while simultaneously looking down at him, a licensed eccentric. Many of the stories about him revelled in his rudeness, apocryphal tales perhaps, much improved in the telling. Anthony Cronin lists those Kavanagh legends, part of Dublin's social currency at the time: 'The story of how Kavanagh had taken off his boots at the public meeting in Trinity College, what he said about her arse to the titled lady who took him to dinner, his reference to the year he had a bath, his approval of the Country Shop as a place to eat because "you got your bellyful there, and it was dainty".'[33]

And yet there was always another side to him. Leland Bardwell, who first met up with Kavanagh in London in the 1950s, was of the opinion that 'what Kavanagh presented as his public persona was the opposite to what he was in reality'.[34]

There were, it seems, many different Kavanaghs – Kavanagh the poet, Kavanagh the drinker, Kavanagh the Dublin character – that made up Kavanagh the man.

Chapter 5

'Alcohol is the worst enemy of the imagination'

Peter, always the more puritanical of the Kavanagh brothers, could be fiercely critical of Patrick's drinking: 'One of the main features of Patrick's character was his intellect. Yet when he entered a pub he would discard it at the door and loll in the confusion and the unknowing of his pub companions, mostly semi-educated who had more time for drinking than for working.'[1]

The Palace Bar in Fleet Street was Dublin's leading literary pub in the 1930s and 1940s though it had been losing its lustre. It was a haunt of R.J. Smyllie and other *Irish Times* journalists and also one of Kavanagh's retreats. Here the great and the good congregated discussing 'such significant matters as George Moore's use of the semi-colon and what English journals paid for book reviews'.[2]

John Ryan recalled: 'The Palace and the Pearl bars were the haunts of the established and the aspiring literati, and the burrows of poetaster and journalist in those days.'[3]

In a well-known Alan Reeve cartoon called Dublin Culture, published by *The Irish Times* in 1940, caricatures of the leading literary lights of the capital at the time are depicted, all of them men. It was unsurprisingly set in the Palace Bar. Patrick Kavanagh is shown standing in the background, his big hands waving in a gesture of disapproval as he appears to be taking his leave.

The main attraction in the pub was Bertie Smyllie, an outsize gentleman with an outsize personality who was editor of *The Irish Times* and who used the Palace as an auxiliary office. Aspiring writers could meet him there, and if they didn't get a job they might at least get a drink. The Palace had the great advantage of proximity to *The Irish Times*' offices on D'Olier Street.

Although the Palace was still the main literary pub in Kavanagh's early years in Dublin, its hey-day, and indeed Smyllie's, had passed. The scene had grown stale. Brian Inglis, one of the younger writers, lamented the passing:

> … occasionally the old Palace atmosphere would be recaptured, usually when some distinguished visitor expressed curiosity about the old days. But even this could be a disillusioning experience. The old Gogarty-style witticisms, brought out for inspection, sounded so much less clever than they had when they were minted, for by 1946 the wisecrack as a form of humour had become standardised, mass-produced on the radio and in films … few of the Palace classics sounded as clever as they had in 1939.[4]

The publication of *The Green Fool* had, according to Anthony Cronin, confirmed Kavanagh's image 'as a naïve and unlettered lyricist at whose expense the Palace Bar could be complacently patronising; nor did his physical appearance when he came to Dublin, and began to try to earn a living there, belie this preconception. Tall, gangling, and with the seeming awkwardness of the countryman in his walk, he became the butt of many Dublin jokes and the comic character in many anecdotes.'[5]

In short, he became a Dublin pub character.

At some point Smyllie, due to some mysterious dispute, took his custom from the Palace and moved it to the Pearl which had the advantage of being even closer to the offices of *The Irish Times*. Most of his cohorts moved with him. As John Ryan described it: 'If Smyllie, wedged in his chair, looking like a stranded bull walrus, a large ball of malt in his chubby hand, even nodded at you – you had it nearly made'.[6]

Honor Tracy wrote of an evening spent there: 'The lounge of the Pearl Bar looked fuller than it was, owing to the presence of the editor of *The Irish Times*. This huge gentleman possessed the gift not only of creating by himself the sense of a party but of bestowing on the whole bar a distinguishing air ... Vast, genial, he would sit there by the hour, his comfortable frame shaking with laughter at the sallies of his companions and draw sagely at his pipe ...'[7]

Tracy recounted an episode with the readily recognisable Kavanagh:

One of Dublin's major poets immediately joined us, with a thirsty look on his face. He was glad to depend on our kindness that evening because the confidence he felt in certain racehorses had turned out to have been misplaced ... the pain of the loss had cast a shadow over his mind and he launched, in his beautiful voice, a diatribe against Ireland and all her works, her passion for mediocrity, her crucifixion of genius: he lamented the passing of his best years among marshmen and Firbolgs: he threatened to shake the dust of her off his feet and to seek his living henceforward in strange places among foreign men.[8]

Dublin literary culture at the time was very male and very drink sodden. Tracy portrayed the denizens of the Pearl:

An Anglo-Irishman of letters with a mad light in his pale eyes, carrying with an air of decision and importance a briefcase that bulged with sandwiches and pyjamas. A literary editor with an air of gentle, refined melancholy about him. More poets. Some playwrights. Lawyers. One gaolbird. Civil Servants. Some of the crowd showed signs of incipient persecution mania, due to their having in fact at one time or another been persecuted. A drunk reeled from one table to the next trying to find someone who would listen once more to the tale of an ancient wrong.[9]

'WHERE THE ELITE MEET'

However, the days of the Palace and the Pearl were passing. The younger poets and writers drank in McDaid's, which was on Harry Street, off Grafton Street, and close to the offices of *Envoy*, to which many of them contributed. Just as the Palace and the Pearl, in their turn, had been an auxiliary office for *The Irish Times*, McDaid's became the place to visit to encounter the *Envoy* set.

An advertisement in *Envoy* at the time portrayed McDaid's, somewhat optimistically, as a place 'where the elite meet' and said that it was a pub where 'the drink is efficacious and the conversation effervescent'. The reality was more mundane. McDaid's was described as having 'an extraordinarily high ceiling and high, almost Gothic, windows in the front wall, with stained-glass borders. The general effect is church-like or tomb-like, according to mood; indeed indigenous folklore has it that it once was a meeting-house for a resurrection sect who liked high ceilings in their places of resort because the best thing of all would be for the end of the world to come during religious service and in that case you would need room to get up steam.'[10]

According to Anthony Cronin: 'McDaid's was never merely

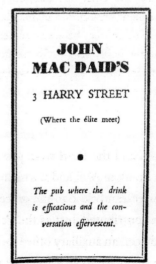

'Where the drink is efficacious and the conversation effervescent.'
McDaid's acted as a second, informal office for Envoy. *Curiously in this advertisement from* Envoy, *the pub is given a different spelling.*

a literary pub. Its strength was always in variety, of talent, class, caste and estate. The divisions between writer and non-writer, bohemian and artist, informer and revolutionary, male and female, were never rigorously enforced; and nearly everybody, gurriers included, was ready for elevation, to Parnassus, the scaffold or whatever.'[11]

The main after-hours drinking den for the literary set was a dingy basement at Fitzwilliam Place, which was called the Catacombs, consisting of a warren of dilapidated rooms, the kitchen, pantry, scullery, broom-cupboard, wine cellar and servants' quarters of a Big House. As Anthony Cronin described it: 'The whole place smelt of damp, decaying plaster and brickwork, that smell of money gone, that was so prevalent in Ireland ... People came and went according to need and circumstance.'[12]

Kavanagh himself had always been aware of the danger of alcohol: 'Wine and women do not go with song. Alcohol is the worst enemy of the imagination. Young writers should keep out of pubs and remember that the cliché way of the artistic life is a lie.'[13]

Kavanagh rarely went to the Catacombs; it was too wild, too bohemian, too debauched for him. Cronin observed: 'Kavanagh drank stout in those days as a staple and was seldom drunk ...' unlike in later years when 'the whiskey had become his master and was cracking the whip'.[14]

'THE DREADFUL DISEASE OF PUNTERITIS'

Patrick Kavanagh did not gamble heavily until 1949. He himself dated the start of his gambling career precisely to 4

June of that year. He had placed a bet on Nimbus, second favourite in the Epsom Derby, in a bookies' shop on Merrion Row. As he described it himself: '… one Derby Day in 1949 I entered a bookies' office for the first time. I went up to the girl at the hole in the partition and shoved in a pound – "On Nimbus," I said. She told me I'd have to write it out on a slip.'

Nimbus won in a photo-finish. The odds were seven-to-one. When he went up to collect his winnings, 'the girl who paid me said I'd be sorry for my win'.[15]

Up to then Kavanagh professed to having had a terrible horror of bookies' shops, thinking they were the haunts of 'degenerate derelicts'. But from then on betting on racing became a time-consuming and expensive addiction, soaking up much of his free time, of which he had an ample supply, and of any spare money, of which he had little. He was an avid reader of newspapers and from then on consumed the racing pages. Hardly a day would go by that he did not have a bet or two, though the amounts wagered were modest. Patrick also added racing to his repertoire of pub topics, passing many an afternoon discussing the likely chances of his chosen steeds.

As John Ryan described it: 'Around about mid-day, Irish or English racing would commence. One would be forgiven for thinking that this marked the serious beginning of the working day, such was the energy with which he and all the other Grafton Street punters threw themselves into the fray … The punters would work on the picking of their nags and return to the pubs at fifteen minute intervals.'[16]

Patrick was not particularly successful with his gambling,

basing many of his selections on little more than superstition or wishful thinking. According to Ryan, however, Kavanagh had 'one long lucky spell that baffled bookmaker and fellow-punter alike. He began to make astonishing sums of money by backing horses that had no form yet consistently won. One bookmaker thought that he had top-secret inside information from the stables and simply refused to take any more bets from him. In fact, all that he had been doing was to back horses with the letter "Z" in their names, regardless of their owner, jockey, pedigree or price.'[17]

However, Kavanagh was not reluctant to share some of his strategies. In an article in *Kavanagh's Weekly* called 'On Punting' he boasted: 'For many years I have been reputed to be a good tipster and I think I am, especially when I am not confused by the dreadful disease of punteritis. Two things are essential for backing winners – a good memory and courage. The good memory is for horses that were proved good a year ago, the courage is to back them in defiance of the racing tipsters.'[18]

Later in the same article he averred: 'The man who would back horses ought to keep a number of principles in mind. It is best to assume that racing is not only on the flat but also on the level. In fact, English racing and to some extent, Irish racing goes extraordinarily close to form. It is not the horses but the backers who go wrong.' Evidently he was less distrustful of horse racing than virtually every other aspect of his life. Nonetheless he was not unaware of the dangers of gambling:

… the world of the punter or the gambler is not a rich imaginative field and the reason for this is that it is a form of disease or of sin … The real immorality of gambling does not consist as certain puritans suggest in the getting of easy money but in the way that gambling is life lived by the sensations.[19]

Chapter 6

'The Casanova of the cinema cafés'

In 1946 Kavanagh was appointed by the *Standard* as their film critic, as successor to Benedict Kiely. Kavanagh had written for the *Standard* for a number of years and Peadar O'Curry, the editor, was a fellow northerner and acquaintance of his, but he was still a curious choice. Perhaps his appointment was at the behest of Patrick's two episcopal patrons, Archbishop McQuaid of Dublin and Archbishop Walshe of Tuam, who he had been pestering to fix him up with a permanent position.

Kavanagh was a most unlikely film critic for the *Standard* because did not have a high opinion of the cinema as an art form, as he announced right from his first review column on 22 February 1946: 'A critic should have an attitude … Scales which are evenly balanced hold nothing … There is no writer more liable to deceive than the one who gives the impression of being impartial. Letting the facts speak for themselves is an immoral principle when we all know that facts and figures can be selected to prove anything.'[1]

After this sturdy statement of intent, Kavanagh went on to list some of his views: 'my taste in films runs to comic stuff …

I used to like gangster films ... I cannot abide musicals ... and above all, I am allergic to hospital pictures in which crowds of young handsome doctors and nurses with masks on are rushing through long corridors to the operating theatre ...'[2]

He had immense disdain for the film industry and Hollywood in particular: 'I may have said this before but I can say it again, that an attempt by a moderately serious writer to make a pair of critical wings from the material provided by the cinema is a hopeless task ... "Trash" is the only word that fairly adequately covers the film business ... God help tomorrow's world if it is going to be anything like the chaos, the jungle of sex-appeal, without literature, without art or without religion which is being created for the simple uneducated by Hollywood.'[3]

He could scarcely believe that a critic could remember ten tolerable films in a year, let alone actually have ten best films. In his next column he was only slightly less dismissive: 'Last week, I was, I am afraid in a rather hypercritical mood. This happens when one suddenly realises the utter futility of the whole cinema world – a world controlled by the most vulgar, least idealistic elements.'[4]

It was a theme he was to return to again: '[To say] that the cinema is as important as books is nonsense. It is as important as the popular trashy books which are written purely for entertainment.'[5]

He also wrote: 'Can it be that Darwin was right after all? The strongest impression left after seeing this week's films and of most weeks during the past few months, is that man has no higher function than the ape. This is Hollywood's consistent theme.'[6]

Kavanagh was aware of the limitations of his position: 'One of the defects implicit in all film criticism is that, nearly all films being low, lewd and illiterate, the critic is inclined to judge by comparisons and not by standards. A film is good because it is not as bad as some other one.'[7]

However, Patrick did not feel all that restricted by his role. He saw his function as a film critic in the broadest possible way, leaving him free to comment on whatever caught his fancy. Some of this writing is very revealing about Kavanagh himself.

On *genius*: 'All great art and great activity of the race of man proceeds from the normal. A genius is an abnormally normal man.'[8]

On *sin*: 'Sin is the flaw in nature, the rot in the seed of the soul through which the buds of Art and of every virtue break into the sunlight. The tree of Christianity has grown out of that decay. Deny Sin; deny Original Sin, and Christianity withers, and withers also all great art. Sin is the source of all great poetry.'[9]

On *truth* and *beauty*: 'Unless something is ugly, nothing is beautiful. Truth is always beautiful, and the portrayal of the glamorous wearies in the end because it is not the truth.'[10]

On *knowledge*: 'Is there a short-cut, an easy way to knowledge? Experience will tell us, I think, that the trouble and pain involved in acquiring knowledge is an essential part of learning. Everyone wants something for nothing these days but we will find that what we have got for nothing is itself nothing. The trouble and pain is the plough that makes the furrow for the seed.'[11]

On *modern culture*: 'With the decay of creative imagination we have conversely the rise of a phoney culture and a phoney society and the veneer of a colossal vanity over imaginative decay.'[12]

On the *artist*: 'The artist is never blinded by love. The poet, in fact, notwithstanding he has been the greatest propagandist for romantic love, is himself incapable of being in love. He is too detached.'

On *fame*: 'It has often occurred to me that men, when they become famous, ought to change their names and begin all over again. Fame is like having a safe seat on a train, we are afraid to get up, to adventure among the other compartments.'[13]

A film musical allowed him to take a swipe at multiple targets: 'There seems to be something in common, between Cubism, Vorticism and all the other "isms" of art, which were the refuges of men and women who had no talent, and jazz music. Values had broken down then. It was the chancers' holiday. The glorious insanity!'[14]

In a review of the film version of Daphne du Maurier's *Hungry Hill* he remarked: 'Why are bad novels the best material for films … film needs action and this it gets in the popular novel and in novels by women, for women are great at writing about ephemeral events as if they were the permanencies of the spirit. They write so fast too that they usually can get these events on paper and published before time takes the ground from under their feet. As a result, women, since they took to writing, always occupy a very large place in the contemporary, literary world and a very small place in the past.'[15]

'LEAVE HIS POETIC SOUL BEHIND'

Unsurprisingly, some of his readership eventually took umbrage at his attitude. Liam Doyle of Arbutus Avenue, Harold's Cross wrote to the *Standard* to ask: 'What is the work of the film critic?' He suggested:

> … perhaps in your reader's interests you might request your film critic to, when he goes to review the films, leave his poetic soul behind … His references some months ago to "drab little Dublin girls" queuing outside … might be tolerated by intelligent people as the mere mouthing of a frustrated male … Surely the job of a film critic is to give an unbiased assessment of the entertainment value of a film. Your critic's reviews, interspersed with his confused reasonings and ramblings on life are hard to understand.[16]

It was not that Kavanagh did not have supporters. Proinsias Ó Conluain wrote the next week in his defence:

> Mr Liam Doyle would have your film critic leave his poetic soul behind him when he enters a cinema. That, in my opinion, would be a pity. We should sympathise, I think, with the poet who has to see, week after week, the unimaginative offerings of Hollywood and should be grateful that he does not bore us with long reviews of tenth-rate films. By ignoring these, or by pungently pointing out their mediocrity, he may save some other poetic souls or even a few prosaic ones like myself from a couple of hours of tedious futility.[17]

In truth, Kavanagh did not need anybody to take up a cudgel on his behalf. He was combative enough on his own. In direct response to Mr Doyle and his 'foolish and pathetic remarks', Kavanagh wrote: 'Our country today is being polluted by film magazines which pander to the drab little girls (and drab little boys) with drab little minds'.[18]

He succeeded in provoking a reaction from an undaunted Mr Doyle who wrote to the *Standard* on 25 April: 'As long as Mr Kavanagh remains in his ivory tower and looks with disdain at the world and its amusements, so long will his film reviews lack that unprejudiced approach vital to proper criticism.'[19]

And again on 9 May Mr Doyle returned to the attack:

> I suggest, Mr Editor, that a film critic can be severe and yet fair, that he can praise and denounce as he thinks fit but that he must be prepared to back up all his assertions with a reasoned and clear argument and that when challenged by a reader he must, instead of abusing him, be big enough to ask himself has he missed the excellence of what he denounced. A critic should be capable of clear thinking and clear writing. His critical utterances should be specific and not just sweeping assertions.[20]

It was not that Kavanagh despised each and every film he saw. If one caught his eye he could be as enthusiastic as any fan. *Lost Weekend* was one such:

> For once Hollywood has left me incapable of criticism … *Lost Weekend* is a most beautiful and moving picture … Ray Milland's performance as the dipsomaniac richly earned him an Academy Award … a still more enchanting performance is that of Jane Wyman's, the virtuous idealistic young girl who sees beneath the emotional storm to the still centre which is the shattered soul

of her lover. Her love and devotion is the very quintessence of virtuous woman.[21]

So impressed was he, that he returned to the film the next week, although he described it as 'not a patch in many ways' on the book on which it was based: 'It is a conflict between good and evil and in the bigger sense of the word it is a far more religious film than many that have to do with purely pious topics such as *Going My Way*.'[22]

And despite his disdain for 'Best of' lists he named *Lost Weekend* as his best film of 1946, 'a moral tale if ever there was one'.

Given his interest in horse racing it was inevitable that he would have strong views on *National Velvet*: 'If you know nothing about racehorses and how they are prepared for their races, and nothing about natural children and their way with horses, you may enjoy *National Velvet* ... The story is of a little English girl, a butcher's daughter who has a great love of horses. She wins one in a raffle and the steed [is] schooled during the winter by Mickey Rooney ... During the winter the horse gets sick and, God forgive me, I hoped he'd die, but no fear, Mickey is better than any vet.'[23]

Patrick used his eminence as a film critic to aid his social life. He brought his dates along with him. As John Ryan put it: '... Kavanagh was by way of being the Casanova of the cinema cafés ... No doubt there were free cups of tea and buns thrown in – as well as the complimentary ticket.'[24] As ever Patrick liked recognition and he was not slow to exploit his status.

On occasion he did write seriously about films. He was

not a fan of Walt Disney and according to his brother said: 'I would like to say with all humility that I have ever found it something of a strain to extract pleasure out of Disney films. Some wonderful virtuosity is to be found in these cartoons, a remarkable inventiveness, but they lack the warmth of imagination. Because it is a technician's world, a world of artistic unfaith, virtuosity is more popular than imagination.'

Kavanagh felt that *Brief Encounters*, though it was banned in Ireland, had some merit: 'While admitting that our Film Censor had hardly any alternative in dealing with a film whose concern is matters of adultery ... *Brief Encounters* has moments of profound pity and some reality ... If this picture is immoral and I think it is, it is because it is insincere. It is a view of a false life, and it is a totally false view of romantic love. For romantic love is not quite the fortuitous happening it is made out to be. There is a considerable element of will about falling in love. There is more of a suicide than accidental death about it.'[25]

In general Kavanagh was more vivid in his scorn than in his praise. *The Yearling* he found a piece of 'unhealthy sentimentality'. *It's a Wonderful Life* was 'about as dull a film as one could fear to run into' and its 'youthful male star is James Stewart and he looks silly'. *Black Narcissus* was 'tripe of the most witless kind', while *The Best Year of Our Lives* was 'long and dull and sentimental'.

As time went on, Patrick, who had never been all that enthusiastic in the first place, grew even more disenchanted and he made little effort to hide it, in fact he flaunted it. Having not reviewed even one film in his column of 16 January 1948, he concluded his piece with the bald statement: 'There are no films this week worth writing about'.[26] In July of the same year, while he did write some perfunctory reviews, he signed off with the assurance: 'Nobody will be any the worse off from never seeing any of the films of this week'.[27]

Quite often he neglected to watch films in their entirety. As his brother told it: 'Ten minutes standing in the back was usually enough time for him to form an opinion of whatever was running on the screen.'[28]

In June 1947 he encountered some trouble over this offhand attitude. He defended his unconventional methods in his column:

> A slight dispute developed between the manager of a cinema and myself this week. The manager suggested that it was impossible for me to know whether a film was bad or good before seeing every foot of it. That is not my view. I believe that one should be able to decide in ten minutes whether a film is worth sitting through. After all, ten minutes of the kind of stuff we generally get spread out before us is more than enough to form an interim judgment.[29]

This was perhaps the last straw for Patrick's long-suffering editor, Peadar O'Curry. His reviewer had admitted that occasionally he didn't watch the entire films, and not only that, there were times he neglected to watch them at all. Peter Kavanagh claimed that now and then when Patrick was out of town, he would write the column that would appear under his brother's name. Peter complained that characteristically, he got no thanks from his brother for this favour.[30]

The end was not long in coming. A month later Kavanagh was replaced as film reviewer, by a more conventional, less controversial columnist who went by the pen-name Scannan. Patrick may have bemoaned his dismissal and the loss of a steady income, but he seemed to have no regrets about not having to review films that he despised. As he put it in later life:

> ... For a number of years I was a film critic. I attended the Irish Film Society shows of a Saturday, and wrote as enthusiastically as the next man ... and that was before I learnt the difficult art of not caring, of having the courage of one's feelings. But it didn't take me quite a while before it came out, the terrible disclosure, that what I thought of most of those foreign films, was what George III thought of Shakespeare, 'Poor stuff but one must not say so' ...[31]

Chapter 7

'Like a monkey house
at feeding time'

As time went on and Patrick gained confidence as a journalist and commentator, he lost whatever reticence he had with regard to his fellow writers. He wrote for *The Bell*, then edited by Peadar O'Donnell, and his literary criticism became more and more outspoken. Kavanagh later explained the development of his views:

> I know that it is possible for a great literary movement to flourish within the context of a nation but the Irish literary movement was not such a one. It took me twenty-five years to discover this, roaring and satirising a lot of poor devils who didn't matter a damn … [it] was in 1947 when I realised for the first time the absurdity and the lie called 'the Irish Literary Movement'.[1]

In a piece in *New Irish Writing*, he re-evaluated the work of Fred Higgins, who had been a friend and mentor in his earlier days in Dublin. Kavanagh explained his misgivings about Higgins' work: 'Writing about F.R. Higgins is a problem

– the problem of exploring a labyrinth that leads nowhere. There is also the problem of keeping oneself from accepting the fraudulent premises and invalid symbols established by the subject. The work of F.R. Higgins is based on an illusion – on a myth in which he pretended to believe. The myth and illusion was "Ireland".'[2]

Kavanagh went on to accuse Higgins of desperately wanting to be a 'droll, gallivanting "Irishman"', and that nearly everything about him would need to be put in inverted commas. Not only that, 'for all his pleasant verse, Higgins was a dabbler … Higgins grew up in an Ireland which had only recently been invented … Personally, Higgins was like his verse. He carried his gallivanting pose into his ordinary life … I hate being cruel to his memory, but I cannot get away from the thought that he never became adult and sincere.'

Kavanagh's assault on the reputation of Higgins was seen at the time as all the more devastating as Higgins was only recently deceased.

One of the other main outlets for Kavanagh's views was *Envoy,* a magazine set up by John Ryan of the Monument Creameries family in 1949. The Ryans owned a chain of cafés and John was an affluent young man on the Dublin scene with literary aspirations of his own. Kavanagh wrote a regular column for the short-lived but influential magazine. Ryan was greatly impressed by the older poet. Kavanagh was allowed to write his opinion pieces, virtually free of editorial interference. He could be as outrageous as he wanted and by this stage he had built up a strong aversion to the Dublin scene. It could be said that he set the tone for *Envoy*'s literary and social criticism.

As Anthony Cronin put it: '*Envoy* itself had come as a godsend to him. When it came along he was totally without literary friends; jobless and ostensibly … penniless … Now he suddenly had a forum where he could speak his mind uninhibitedly.'[3]

The journal provided a mouthpiece where Kavanagh could attack those institutions of the establishment that he had grown to despise: Radio Éireann, the Abbey Theatre and the writers of the Celtic Revival. He saw a lack of creativity all around him: 'To be successful one should avoid originality at all costs. How often have I observed cunning young men on the climb repeating carefully verbatim the old clichés which had served others before.'[4]

In the last issue of *Envoy* John Ryan boasted:

> We afforded Patrick Kavanagh an opportunity of pouring fire and destruction on the heads of that untalented body of poetasters who are bringing Irish writing into disrepute beyond our shores, and who are seeking to divert the attention of our intelligent reading-public from whatever is valuable in Irish letters today.
>
> … Few people at present appreciate the service that Patrick Kavanagh has rendered to the cause of truth in Ireland. He has helped to liberate young writers, early in their careers, from misjudgments and restrictive influences.[5]

Not everybody was quite so impressed with Kavanagh's journalism. As Hubert Butler put it at the time: 'Writers and artists are children when it comes to politics. What can you expect? That is especially true of poets and in an over-stable society maybe their childishness has value. It is like a window pane broken in a stuffy room … it might be helpful to conduct a postmortem on the defunct monthly *Envoy*, for this was the organ of Ireland's rebellious writers. We might learn what they were rebelling against, and if and why the rebellion failed.'[6]

Butler argued that the worth of any Irish magazine should not be judged by the length of its survival: 'An Irish journal is like a sortie from a besieged city. Its effects cannot be measured by its duration.'[7] One of the major achievements of *Envoy* was to have given Kavanagh the opportunity of serving the cause of truth in Ireland and of scourging the untalented, 'who are bringing Irish writing into disrepute beyond our shores'. Butler goes on to remark that in the last issue of the magazine, 'the editor and Mr Kavanagh complimented each other in having done a good job!'

Furthermore, Butler asserts: '*Envoy* had something serious to say. Perhaps it was the very urgency of the message that made the messenger so breathless … *Envoy* was a good and gallant paper and its death is a tragedy.'[8]

Butler was, however, particularly critical of Kavanagh's political and social journalism: '… it is the conflict within the writer's own mind which is demoralising. Mr Kavanagh's mind, when he abandons poetry and fiction, is like a monkey house at feeding time … Mr Kavanagh is highly gifted and the fact that he has to tell us so himself is in our grudging society no proof of the contrary.'[9]

As time went on in the 1940s and early 1950s Kavanagh fell out with most of his previous mentors, including Peadar O'Donnell, editor of *The Bell*, and Frank O'Connor, the original 'bun man', who he now condemned as yet another fake: 'Frank O'Connor is often to be seen coming out of bun-shops on

Grafton Street, and dreaming into the sky-line of Graftonia, but one has the unholy feeling that he is not a true bun-man … O'Connor is a great story-teller but he lacks heart. His laughter is hollow, and hollowing …'[10]

If he was cutting in public, he was even less circumspect in private. He told his brother that Smyllie, the editor of *The Irish Times*, was 'a gasbag of no ability', his reason being: 'I am beginning to guess that he didn't exactly love myself, never gave me a job.'[11]

In 'The Paddiad', he also took swing at the Pearl Bar set:

> In the corner of a Dublin pub,
> This party opens – blub-a-blub,
> Paddy Whiskey, Rum and Gin,
> Paddy Three Sheets in the wind

All these 'Paddies' were, if not readily identifiable, recognisable as types. Maurice Walsh, M.J. McManus, Robert Farren and Austin Clarke were among those suspected of inspiring Kavanagh's venom:

> Paddy of the Celtic Mist,
> Paddy Connemara West,
> Chestertonian Paddy Frog,
> Croaking nightly in the bog

Based on Alexander Pope's *The Dunciad*, Kavanagh's 'Paddiad' is an indication that the poet had lost whatever remnants of tolerance he had for the literary scene in Dublin, burning his bridges with glee. The poem was a product, not just of his contempt, but also of the frustration that Kavanagh was feeling. He could not make a living in Dublin, he was almost fifty, still barely getting by, one step away from poverty, having to scrape and bow to his perceived inferiors.

In later life, Kavanagh spoke of this time: 'I was a man bursting with belief in myself, I was bursting with belief in my point of view and the job was to get a forum for that belief. I was arrogant and satirical of fools and didn't realise that such a man could not be safely employed.'[12]

Brian Inglis was of the opinion that Kavanagh had not fulfilled his early promise: 'Patrick Kavanagh had seemed to have notable possibilities ... but having left his Monaghan farm behind him and written its memory out of his system, he allowed resentments to grip him ... venting them on sycophants who liked him the better for his savage contempt of them ... and his verse never recovered its early impact.'[13]

Kavanagh's critical impulse was not selective. He could be just as hard on himself and told Anthony Cronin that his own book, *The Green Fool*, was 'a ridiculous book by a bollocks, a bollocks who knew nothing about himself, let alone anyone else'.[14]

Chapter 8

'And I had loved not as I should, a creature made of clay'

According to Peter Kavanagh, not all Patrick's time was spent writing or looking for a job: a large portion of it was spent searching for the woman of his dreams. He wanted 'a lady who would always be beautiful and enthusiastic, and never grouchy or sick. Meanwhile he would be satisfied with young bouncy girls.'[1]

Peter went on to say: 'Yet he was no libertine. He needed female companionship. The light that emanated from an attractive girl was part of the poetic flame. He loved the ideal more than the reality and this kept him in a state of constant excitement.'[2]

Kavanagh seemed to prefer the company of women to that of men, perhaps because he did not see them as artistic equals. He could relax with them and not have to be competitive. Having been brought up in a house with six sisters he was comfortable in the company of women.

Kavanagh had a poor view of women as creative artists: 'Little girls who should be at home nursing babies or cooking the dinner and shadowy journalists from the continent of Europe are to be found within the covers of every Catholic paper you take up.'[3]

Kavanagh had quite definite opinions about women in general and could be spectacularly misogynistic: 'Women are wise in their generation and their instincts. But when they abandon their perceiving bodies for their soon dried-up brains they become intolerable. The body with its feelings, its instincts, provides women with a source of wisdom but they lack the analytic detachment to exploit it in literature.'[4]

To judge by his early poetry, Patrick had a romantic nature, in theory if not in practice. As his biographer Antoinette Quinn put it: 'He had been very susceptible to the charms of pretty women from puberty and regularly fell in love … never declaring his feelings, merely worshipping from afar'.[5]

In conservative, rural Monaghan in the 1930s Kavanagh would have had few outlets for his amorous yearnings. Having arrived in Dublin in 1939, aged thirty-five, he was in many ways adolescent in his attitudes. He may have been socially awkward, but his outgoing nature meant that he was never afraid to make contact with the young women he met on the street or in the cafés of Dublin. He seemed to have a preference for beautiful, intelligent, middle-class ladies. Often they had a love of literature and usually they would be a good deal younger than him. As Antoinette Quinn states: 'Kavanagh preferred to court women who were not real artists and did not pit their intellect against his.'[6]

In 1944 Kavanagh fell for a medical student called Hilda Moriarty, inspiration for one of his best remembered poems,

'On Raglan Road'. She was undoubtedly beautiful, she came from an affluent background and she had a retinue of admirers. Patrick had a chivalrous nature when it came to women and he always liked to be helpful, seeing himself as a sort of courtly suitor. In a letter to Archbishop McQuaid he endeavoured to find a place for Hilda in the Holy Child Hostel. He described her as a 'charming, virtuous' girl. As he put it: 'I should be very pleased to be the means of doing good to one who has done good to me.'[7]

Hilda seems to have been enthralled by his poetry and his conversation, though it is unlikely that she ever took him seriously as a romantic suitor. Like many of the young women who caught his eye, she seems to have been simultaneously flattered and alarmed by his intense attentions. She did, however, treat him with a delicate compassion. Anthony Cronin recounts how he would see them 'walking along the street together or drinking coffee in Mitchels together'.[8]

Dublin could be a small village, made even smaller when it came to the haunts of the middle class and Patrick would often loiter in places where he might 'accidentally' meet his beloved. 'On Raglan Road' gives details of the outcome of one such encounter that had his love fleeing from him:

> On a quiet street where old ghosts meet I see her walking now,
> away from me so hurriedly my reason must allow,
> that I had wooed not as I should, a creature made of clay ...

The poem in its initial incarnation was called 'Dark Haired Miriam ran away'. According to his brother, Patrick called it this in order to disguise its provenance and lessen his (and Hilda's) embarrassment. Miriam was in fact the name of one of Peter's girlfriends at the time.[9]

Benedict Kiely tells how he was perhaps the first to hear the new poem, in the offices of the *Standard*: 'He had it written out rather badly in pencil', on a scrap of brown paper. Kavanagh asked Kiely if it could be sung to the air of *Fáinne Geal an Lae* (*The Dawning of the Day*) and the two of them tried it out. As Benedict put it: 'We raised our voices together in a cacophony that fortunately nobody was there to hear. We must have been terrible to listen to.'[10]

Patrick was bitter and hurt by Hilda's eventual rejection of him: 'Hilda wanted a man with a future, the sure sign of a shallow mind,' he told his brother. He recounted meeting her on the street having heard that she was going to be married. She had her hair up, he recalled. She didn't need it down any more. The hunt was over, she had found herself a suitable prospective husband: 'She ran into me the other day all smiles looking for congratulations. Of course I said everything proper. Not interested enough to say else.'[11]

This was fairly typical of Patrick's misadventures when it came to women, but it was one of the more passionate incidents. As he said to Peter: 'it was a very bad dose, even though it was submerged'.[12]

His intensity, not to mention his down-at-heel appearance, lack of money and indifference to personal hygiene, may have repelled potential girlfriends. Patrick was also unrealistic in his expectations. He wanted these young women to look after him. Though obviously older and presumably more experienced,

Patrick sought out younger, supportive, surrogate mothers. He saw women as providers. As Antoinette Quinn writes: 'desire is seen as inseparable from dependency, even infantilisation'.[13] Kavanagh's apparent helplessness when it came to financial or domestic matters brought out the protective nature of these kindly young women. However, they did not see him as marriage material, which is what he desperately wanted to be.

Kavanagh wanted security but he had unrealistic and over-optimistic expectations of how to achieve this. Antoinette Quinn believes: 'His longing for a home was closely connected with his longing for personal security in the form of steady employment or a regular pay packet.'[14]

There was also an element of arrogance in his attitude to women. He did not see them as his equal. He was a poet, an artist, and they were not. As he put it in 'On Raglan Road': 'I gave her gifts of the mind I gave her the secret sign that's known/to the artists who have known the true gods of sound and stone/and word and tint ...'

It was rather like his attitude to work; he liked the idea of a relationship but was less comfortable with the reality. It was a curious mix of public arrogance and private vulnerability. As the writer Leland Bardwell put it: '... in person he was cosy and loving. He loved all women and believed that God must be a woman.'[15]

Despite this belief, there is no doubt that Kavanagh held peculiar views that coloured his attitude towards women:

I also discovered that the better-looking women are, the wiser they are. There is probably a reason for this; women are magnets which draw wisdom, and they draw their wisdom through men, so it follows that the more attractive a woman is the more she is likely to draw wisdom; for in the first place she can afford to be selective and have as male friends only fairly intelligent ones.[16]

Fellow poet Robert Greacen was of the opinion that Kavanagh 'liked women to be what was then called "womanly" and remarked of a girlfriend of mine that she was "a real woman". No higher praise could he give.'[17]

Many people assumed 'The Great Hunger' to be auto-biographical in a way that it was not. Patrick Maguire was not Patrick Kavanagh. 'No hope, no lust' was not how Kavanagh lived his life. In fact the opposite could be stated. Patrick always had hope and he always had lust. He was more prone to romantic disappointment than to frustration. As Anthony Cronin describes it: 'In terms of the company and conversation of women and the proofs of affection and understanding he required, he didn't do too badly, even at the worst of times. By comparison with the accepted idea of his relationship with the opposite sex in those years and indeed by comparison with the love-life of most of the people … his private life was that of a pampered and indulged figure in what almost amounted to a harem.'[18]

'WOMEN FOR PLEASURE AND WOMEN FOR USE'

Cronin recalls how Kavanagh 'used to distinguish in his cups between "women for pleasure and women for use". This was a mere boast, but perhaps it concealed a more important dichotomy of feeling. There were women for being fond of and

women for loving, and loving may have been a very remote
and sacred ceremony to be performed before a very high and
sacred altar.'[19]

His secretive nature meant that he often had more than one
relationship on the go at any one time. These young women
seldom knew that they were not the one and only.

An account of a typical Kavanagh relationship is given by
May O'Flaherty of Parsons Bookshop:

> Patrick was so unconventional and independent he would have
> been a hard man to please. Though he was a very private person,
> he couldn't help telling us sometimes about his latest love and he
> once introduced us to Deirdre Courtney, a very nice person and
> a member of the Legion of Mary. They met outside the shop a
> few times and walked along the canal, but she was far too young
> for him and it didn't endure. I heard the last straw was when he
> agreed to go on a pilgrimage to Lough Derg with her but didn't
> turn up.[20]

Miss O'Flaherty held the view that 'if he'd had a more stable
life, it might have saved him from all those terrible medical
problems' he was to suffer from in later life.

Kavanagh had an ambiguous attitude to the passion he
inspired in others. As he himself argued in one of his film
columns in the *Standard*: 'Each man tries to kill the thing that
loves him. To be loved is to have power over the lover, and to
have power is dangerous.'[21]

Chapter 9

'The old foolishness'

Early in the spring of 1952 Peter Kavanagh returned from America, 'not exactly a celebrity but not a failure either', as he himself put it. Patrick, however, was 'at low ebb, he had no means of support, visible or invisible. No one would publish a line he wrote.'[1] This was somewhat of an exaggeration but there was an element of truth in it. His two favourite magazines, first *The Bell* and then *Envoy*, the main vehicles for his writings at the time, had both folded.

On his arrival back in Ireland Peter found Patrick 'in poverty – almost starving in fact – but bursting with ideas for which he had no outlet. He suggested that with my savings we might start a weekly newspaper.'[2]

Peter was less enthusiastic; it was, after all, his money that would be needed to set up the magazine. As he told a friend at the time: 'My brother is at me again, pressuring me to start a weekly … it would be a terrible strain for me with Patrick dominating everything'. But Patrick was 'bursting with ideas that he wanted to propagate. He longed for a forum where he could speak without editorial control.'[3]

KAVANAGH'S WEEKLY

A JOURNAL OF LITERATURE AND POLITICS

Vol. 1. No. 1.	SATURDAY, APRIL 12, 1952	SIXPENCE

CONTENTS:

The first edition of Kavanagh's Weekly *hit the streets in April 1952.*
Kavanagh's Weekly *lasted for thirteen eventful issues.*

John Ryan, by no means an unbiased observer, as he had been editor of *Envoy*, was of the opinion that what Kavanagh 'had achieved in the span of *Envoy*'s life was to be the most sustained, confident and lucid period of creative writing of his career. Indeed when the magazine finally folded such was the momentum that had carried him, he simply had to replace it with something else and that something else became *Kavanagh's Weekly*.'[4]

The plan was for an eight-page magazine, a relatively small project one would think. They set a very ambitious target to print and sell 3,000 copies each week. But as they found out straightaway, it was a much bigger job than they had anticipated. The *Weekly* was subtitled 'A Journal of Literature and Politics', which gives some indication of its priorities. They had no intention of confining it to literature; their horizons were much wider. The problem was they had no business plan as regards income, advertising, distribution or even contributions. Not only that, the filling of those eight pages was a far more arduous task than they had foreseen. Most of the content ended up having to be written by the two brothers themselves, often under pseudonyms so as to disguise this paucity. They also had another good reason to use pen-names – the controversial nature of some of the articles.

Peter later wrote: 'It was an immense job for two people to write and distribute a weekly of 10,000 words. We received almost no help from anyone. Some contributions came in but they were mostly of little or no interest … As well as writing, I designed the format, supervised the printing and went around on my bicycle distributing the paper.'[5]

Kavanagh's Weekly had an amateurish look to its layout. There were no illustrations, just a simple three column arrangement of large blocks of text. Peter did the layout, learning as he went. Right from the beginning they had virtually no income, either from advertising or from subscriptions, nor had they any real prospect of income in the future. The brothers put an advertisement for Devin Adair, Peter's American publishers, in the first issue, but that was for design reasons, to fill a blank space on a page that was left when the *Weekly* was about to go to print. Things did not improve: 'No advertiser would dare touch us except Victor Waddington, the art dealer.'[6]

The *Weekly* deliberately set out to be controversial. It was an irreverent medium for the brothers' views on the middle-class values of the Irish nationalist establishment. They attacked mediocrity where they saw it, in art, in literature, in politics;

all the sacred cows of the Irish middle class – the civil service, tourism, broadcasting and the Irish language. They abhorred the materialism of the new Ireland and they criticised what they saw as the conservative unthinking religion. The Department of External Affairs, Radio Iran [Radio Éireann], *The Irish Times*, the Irish Hospital Sweepstakes, the Defence Forces and especially de Valera and the Fianna Fáil Party all came in for a lash. The Irish language movement, pretension in the arts, pomposity and self-importance in politics, also found themselves mocked in the paper. They also lamented the high level of emigration asking: 'Why are people leaving the countryside in their thousands? They go to England where conditions are extremely bad. What they are seeking is the enthusiasm for life.'[7]

The tone of the magazine was lively, often angry and sometimes incoherent. It was clearer what the brothers were against than what they were for. The two brothers attacked Ireland's establishment with impunity and glee. In the first issue Peter, using the pseudonym John L. Flanagan, used an incident he knew of to attack the behaviour of some of the Irish diplomatic service abroad: 'The consular official never kept the appointment … but explained … that he had been out to a private party the previous evening, had got blind drunk, stayed overnight and continued drinking the next day completely oblivious of every appointment.'[8]

In the lead editorial in the first issue Patrick lamented the victory of mediocrity:

All the mouthpieces of public opinion are controlled by men whose only qualification is their inability to think … being stupid

and illiterate is the mark of respectability and responsibility ...
As with sin, mediocrity is never pernicious until we begin to call
it statesmanship and common sense.[9]

His attack on mediocrity even extended to the Defence
Forces. He said: 'They would certainly be good at defending a
field of turnips against an invasion of crows'.[10] *The Irish Times*
was described as a 'pit of turgidity' and was on 'the side of the
dullest, deadest elements in the country'. Its Saturday book-
page was 'a square of flooring timber that would, if usable,
advance any building scheme'.

The Arts Council and other government cultural bodies
also came in for criticism: 'Men who in a well-ordered society
would be weeding a field of potatoes or cutting turf in a bog
are now making loud pronouncements on art.'

About Radio Éireann Kavanagh remarked: 'It is true that
radio everywhere is more or less a pitiful thing ... But in Ireland
the radio is a farce of a most unamusing kind ... at the present
time it is a useless branch of the sub-civil service where a large
number of people lie low and draw their salaries.'[11]

The Abbey Theatre fared no better: 'As for what is called
the Abbey School of Acting this was – and still is – one of the
worst afflictions we have endured: that and the language used
by the Abbey playwrights.'[12]

Furthermore Kavanagh contended: 'Compulsory Irish
should end. Any man who looks the facts in the face knows
that the revival of Irish has been a complete failure and even
worse; it has in fact killed what little hope there was for the
survival of the spirit of the language.'[13]

On public life in general Kavanagh remarked: 'We would like to see published annually the bank accounts and investments of all our public men and patriots. This would give us an idea of the motives that inspired these men, how far it was selfless or how far it had to do with feathering of nests.'[14]

In the following month's edition he went on to say: 'The business, civil service, political world is a conspiracy against the common people, and the object of the newspapers, which are owned by this section of the community, is to offer the common people something to distract them from the true state of affairs.'[15]

However, by issue four a serious problem had revealed itself:

> To our readers: This journal is a non-profit-making venture, there are no rich backers behind it. To survive it must get the co-operation and support of its readers. Our first problem is distribution. Would readers therefore, in certain areas, offer themselves as distributors? If so would they communicate with the publisher and arrange to take a certain number of copies each week?[16]

May O'Flaherty of Parsons Bookshop was happy to help out by stocking the *Weekly*: 'We were pleased to help and we were the first port of call on Peter's distribution round.'[17]

Perhaps a fortnightly magazine or a monthly or better still a quarterly would have been a superior arrangement, giving them enough time to produce a more organised paper. As it was, they sold fewer copies than they had predicted. As Patrick put it: 'Dublin is a city of much talk but little action'.[18]

Despite problems with distribution, the brothers were determined to continue producing the *Weekly*. Political, social and economic matters dominated the paper. Peter's views perhaps overrode those of Patrick who always had the tendency to be influenced by those in his immediate circle. Patrick's lack of formal education combined with his open, inquiring mind, often resulted in a certain vague style.

The brothers, by this time, had adopted a siege mentality. The whole world was against them, especially that conglomerate body, the Irish establishment. They reinforced each other, in their social isolation, living together in the flat on Pembroke Road, working flat-out full-time on the *Weekly*. Entrenched in a world of their own ideas, they viewed the class system in Ireland as the enemy:

> There is a class called the bourgeoisie and this class is the enemy of every fine and enlarging idea. That class has got a tremendous grip on the twenty-six counties; in Dublin they operate almost as a secret society; they are interlocked among the directorates of various large companies; touch one and you touch them all. The bourgeoisie is almost entirely the work of that noted American, Eamon de Valera.[19]

By the fifth issue they endeavoured to defend themselves against accusations of negativity: 'Once again it is necessary to comment on this notion about our "destructiveness", our "bitterness". Society here is adolescent and cannot distinguish moral indignation from bitterness. In fact the enmity and opposition to our "bitterness" which we have come up against is as bitter and as ugly a thing as we have ever encountered.'[20]

They were determined to go down fighting. But the brothers' distribution network depended on Peter and his bicycle. According to Peter, Eason's were initially wary of distributing the first issue: 'Old Bob Eason didn't like what he saw and refused to distribute it until he had thoroughly read the issue and had a lawyer pass it as free of libel ... While Eason was thinking over the matter I started off on my bicycle with a large bundle of the *Weekly* on the carrier ... I called on every newspaper shop in Dublin ...' This lack of income was compounded by the fact that the *Weekly* carried virtually no advertisements. It was essentially a loss maker from day one.[21]

Myles na gCopaleen contributed some articles, but Peter regarded them as being of very poor quality. In later issues Myles also chipped in with a number of letters, characteristically truculent, disagreeing with the *Weekly*'s attitude to the Irish language and also pointing out in his inimitable pedantic style, some misspellings in the paper: '*Kavanagh's Weekly* does not attack the right people. Maybe its armour is weak ... There is endless opportunity. Will *Kavanagh's Weekly* have a go ... I'm afraid I must say this. They won't be let.'[22]

The list of things that was wrong with Ireland according to *Kavanagh's Weekly* was long and scathing. Included in the list was: her geographical position – too far west of European culture, resulting in a delay of about a generation in the impact of new ideas; the climate, which accounts for most of our bad humour; an excess of piety and insufficient charity; the Sunday drinking hours, designed to prevent a drinker, in the cities, from having his dinner and tea with the family; the pure, beautiful young women who were set by God in Ireland to tempt, taunt and thwart the frustrated men there.[23] The list was, not coincidentally, thirty-two long.

The brothers quickly came to realise that the magazine was 'a treadmill of their own making'.[24] When John Ryan asserted that 'as contributors were not paid he ended up by writing the entire paper, including the letters-to-the-editor, himself', he was only slightly exaggerating.[25]

However, it was not all earnestness in the *Weekly*. A gentler form of ridicule was the regular column compiled by Patrick, called *The Old Foolishness*. It consisted of newspaper extracts. He had always been a voracious reader of Irish newspapers and magazines and he simply reproduced any absurdities that caught his eye. Patrick reprinted the snippets without comment:

Mr Patrick Ivory, his father, said: 'I don't think it was the Guards who hit him. He has been out of hospital since Sunday.'

The book as a whole is so entertaining, so gracious in its English as befits a writer who was a journalist before he took to the law.

Death-watch beetles in Senate Chamber.

Regarding the question of erecting two public lavatories in the town ... Mr Cahill said: 'I don't know of any urban area in the county with a ladies' and gent's lavatory. You cannot have a low rate and go in for those high-brow schemes.'

The man in charge does not want to fool you. He wants to save you from yourselves. – Dan Breen

Sixteen girls at Shannon are making enough leprechauns to net the airport thousands of dollars this year.

Give the foreigner Irish pure and undiluted at every turn. He will respect us the more for it.

We want freedom, we want the national language restored and, of course, we want the unity of our country in order to have freedom. After that we are interested in the general well-being of the people. – de Valera

Patrick even instigated some mock competitions for their readership, parodying the type of competition that the Irish Sunday papers ran. In the very first issue the *Weekly*'s 'fashion correspondent' announced: 'We regret to say we lost the picture which goes with our mannequin parade competition. However, we are going on without it. Here are the letters that marked the different pictures:

L D A P R O V C Z I E W Y

Write down these letters in the order of your choice … The prize is a splendid atom-powered 1996 Ford. It will be on view on the stage of the rebuilt Abbey Theatre on opening night.'

Given that they had hardly any readership and next to no money, it was just as well the competitions were bogus.

The *Weekly* reported that there was a scarcity of wild goats in Ireland, which was worrying the organisers of the Puck Fair: 'Have the buck-goats emigrated to England because of the strict code of morality here?' Perhaps the Arts Council could lend a hand.[26]

By issue number twelve the end was in sight. They announced that the next issue would be the last: 'If, however, we receive in the meantime, a sum of £1,000 or upward, we will distribute next week's issue in the ordinary way and continue publishing *Kavanagh's Weekly*.'

Kavanagh's Weekly's eventful run finished with the thirteenth issue. It had lasted from 12 April to 5 July 1952, thirteen frantic weeks. Patrick rationalised its demise: 'Our main problem was two-headed. First, there is an absence of writers and secondly the absence of an audience.'[27]

So that was the prognosis: they had neither enough writers nor enough readers. All Peter's savings were gone. But Patrick still felt it was worth it:

> The editor of this paper has learned a very useful lesson from his experience with this weekly paper. For more than ten years, he had suffered from the delusion that he had in Dublin a large body of friends of a special kind ... They kept telling him to stick to ballads, to what he knew of country life, but not to start talking about such abstruse matters as money and politics.[28]

He concluded on a philosophical note: 'The only power that is worthwhile is knowledge, knowledge of oneself and of other people in relation to oneself'.[29]

Unsold copies of *Kavanagh's Weekly*, of which there were many, were burned in the flat on Pembroke Road. On 11 July, Eason's bookshops sent back 400 copies.[30] As John Ryan described it: 'The conflagration continued for many a week. Mighty plumes of black smoke ascended during the day while by night the Pembroke sky-line was an orange glow ...'[31] In later years, looking back on the episode Patrick stated: 'This was during the final years of my belief in belief and my belief in Ireland as a spiritual entity'.[32]

The brothers, wrapped up in the production of their paper, probably overestimated its effect. The establishment hardly seemed to notice and it failed to provoke the reaction that the brothers had hoped for. The *Weekly* was hardly mentioned in any of the other newspapers at the time. The *Sunday Press* did take a swipe at Peter Kavanagh in its 20 April edition, but it was over something Peter had written previously in America.

Kavanagh's Weekly carried no hard news or investigative articles. It was filled almost entirely with commentary pieces and no matter how vividly they were written they were mainly propaganda, manifestos for a political party that never was.

Kavanagh with Anthony Cronin (right) *and John Ryan* (centre) *on Bloomsday 1954.* Courtesy of the National Library of Ireland

Chapter 10

'A noisy, anti-intellectual, ultra-nationalist rag'

The Leader had been in circulation since 1900, set up by D.P. Moran, a self-described 'converted West Briton'. He launched the magazine as an 'independent weekly review, written from first to last from exclusively Irish standpoints'.[1] It was first published in September 1900 and 'enjoyed a remarkable success, driven by Moran's scathing and outspoken commentaries on events. Unabashedly nationalist and Catholic in tone he enjoyed a gift for self-projection and awareness that a good dispute caught attention and raised sales.'[2]

Moran strongly promoted Catholicism, the revival of the Irish language and 'the encouragement of Irish industry and concerted action against imported smut ...'[3] He was seen as an aggressive and articulate exponent of a Catholic, Gaelic vision of Irish identity, summed up in his slogans 'Irish Ireland' and 'The Gael must be the element that absorbs'.[4] As Brian Inglis put it, Moran believed 'that what was distinctive about the

Kavanagh was in London when the offending article was published.

Irish character must be kept distinctive'.[5] The great connecting link was the Gaelic tongue. The language had to be revived.

In the Golden Jubilee issue of October 1950, its editorial claimed:

> *The Leader* was established to combat those forces that would destroy the nation, and it raised its voice fearlessly against those who aped, like slaves, their British 'betters' in education, manners and morals. *The Leader* proclaimed a comprehensive nationalism based not on the bombast of politicians but on a love of the traditions and lore of our people and on a healthy self-respect for our own abilities in industrial and commercial affairs.[6]

On D.P. Moran's death in 1936 the magazine continued on in the ownership of his children. It had been in decline since independence in 1922, after which event it was increasingly irrelevant. Peter Kavanagh, by no means an unbiased judge, thought it a partly defunct paper that had outlived its usefulness: '… a noisy, anti-intellectual, ultra-nationalist rag'.[7]

The Leader's subtitle was 'Current Affairs – Literature – Politics – Art and Industry', which gives some indication of its priorities. According to Brian Inglis, a regular contributor to the magazine in the early 1950s, it was a 'journal of opinion catering for liberal Catholic opinion and for language lovers'.[8] He admitted that 'the circulation of *The Leader* was very small … though it was read by Catholic bishops and parish priests'.[9]

In an effort to improve its fortnightly circulation, *The Leader* had started a 'profile' section on Irish public figures in early 1952. The first personality covered was the academic Alfred O'Rahilly, next was R.M. Smyllie, editor of *The Irish Times*, then C.S. Andrews who was head of Bord na Móna at the time, and then Joseph Brennan of the Central Bank.

The profiles proved a success for *The Leader* and each issue had a trailer for the next profile. The Earl of Wicklow, Seán MacBride, Jack B. Yeats, Professor E.J. Conway and Michael MacLiammor were also profiled. Looking at the professions of those covered gives some indication of the interest of *The Leader*'s readership: academics, public servants, politicians, the majority of them male. In the 11 October 1952 issue Patrick Kavanagh became the subject of the tenth profile. When

Kavanagh's profile was published *The Leader* printed some fly-posters to publicise it. Kavanagh's solicitors spent some time trying to lay their hands on one of those posters before the case went to trial, but to no avail.

There was some similarity in the lay-out of *The Leader* and *Kavanagh's Weekly*, but one big difference was that *The Leader* carried a large number of advertisements in its twenty-four pages. From its inception *The Leader* had been well supported by Ireland's Catholic, nationalist business class and this had been maintained over the years despite the decline in the magazine's popularity.

In the issue in which the profile of Kavanagh was carried, there were large advertisements for, amongst others: New Ireland Assurance, Irish Hospital Sweepstakes, Johnston, Mooney & O'Brien, D.B.C. Cakes, Hibernian Insurance, Theatre Royal, Providence Woollen Mills, Irish Shipping Ltd., National City Bank, ESSO, An Gum and Comhlucht Siucre Éireann.

Patrick was in England at the time but the article was brought to his attention by Elinor O'Brien, a neighbour and friend from Dublin who had been trusted to mind the flat in Pembroke Road while Patrick was away. Two weeks later, still in England, Patrick wrote to Peter outlining his determination to move against the publisher, the printer and the distributor of *The Leader*:

> I am sending you the article ... Rory O'Connor is my solicitor and my counsel are Sir John Esmonde, SC, T.A. Doyle, BL ... The view is that I cannot lose the action and may well get substantial damages ... Brian Inglis and a fellow named James Meehan, a

friend of Ben Kiely, are involved in *The Leader* and they have it
in for me over *K*[avanagh]'s *Weekly* which did so much damage
to their cause … had we been able to continue we would have
conquered the country … we did some good … There is much
speculation over who wrote the profile on me. I suspected Inglis
but a lot think it Tommy Woods … Only the O'Brien one sent
me the copy I might not have seen it for months.[10]

Peter was of the opinion that while the article was super-
ficially friendly, underneath 'ran a vein of malice, fury and
resentment'.[11]

As Miss O'Flaherty of Parsons Bookshop recalled:
'Patrick was very upset by the profile which he saw as part
of a campaign to belittle him. We all agreed that it was very
hurtful. But, like many of our customers, we thought he might
have expected something like that after all the attacks in his
own paper. Some suggested that the article was no more than
the normal jealous banter between poets and writers and that
Patrick should ignore it and get on with his work.'[12]

However, it was not in Patrick's nature to let such public
affront pass. As another worker from Parsons put it: 'Patrick
could be irascible and touchy and would easily take offence.
He could spot phoniness and pretension a mile off … He was
very sensitive to any slight, real or imagined …'[13]

The Leader had replied to the first letter from Kavanagh's
solicitors with questions of clarifications of their own. They
wanted to know what exactly was objectionable about the
article. But by then Patrick had already decided to pursue the
action. In November he wrote to Peter: 'At all events I am
confident of getting anything from 500 pounds upwards … I

don't think they'll let it go to court … I mean business and am determined to smash them …'[14]

However, the nearer the date got, the more nervous Kavanagh became. His brother recalls: 'Patrick expressed a willingness to settle for nominal damages and an apology but the defence would have none of it. They were out for revenge.'[15]

There was some uncertainty about pursuing Eason's as part of the action. Sir John Esmonde, senior counsel for the plaintiff in his 'Advice of Proofs' had asked if Eason's were warned by Kavanagh's solicitor that there was libellous material in a magazine they were distributing and that Eason's had disregarded the warning.[16] Rory O'Connor, Kavanagh's solicitor, had on 18 January 1954, just weeks before the trial was due to start, written to Kavanagh: 'Please let me know … particulars of the warning given to Eason's and particulars of the evidence we will be able to give that Eason's disregarded the warning.'[17] Kavanagh and his counsel later decided to omit Eason's from the lawsuit, probably due to lack of proof against them. This would simplify matters, there would be one less lawyer ready to cross-examine Patrick.

Patrick wrote to his brother seeking support: 'Dear Peter, my law action comes up next week … p.s. I'll need you over.'[18] Despite asking for his brother's support, Patrick had some doubts about the effect Peter would have on proceedings. Peter had a reputation as a firebrand. Patrick needed his backing but at the same time feared that any mention of Peter's journalism would weaken the case. He feared that all those controversial opinions that Peter had expressed so forcefully in *Kavanagh's*

Weekly would be used against him in the case. Patrick wrote: 'I can defend my own point of view but I cannot defend yours ...Your writing will ruin me.'[19] He was now seriously worried that the case would go to court. However, he was not going to back down. He would see it through.

Chapter 11

'Odium, hatred, ridicule and contempt'

Put an Irishman on the spit and you can always get another Irishman to turn him.

George Bernard Shaw

On the day of the trial, to give Patrick a better appearance, Peter loaned him his raincoat. In no way grateful, Patrick refused to be photographed with his brother. Peter blamed Patrick's retinue of mentors who had advised him to distance himself from his brother. He did not wish to be seen in public with him: 'I found him to be in a state of great agitation … He had been brainwashed by his pub friends. They had built up a new character for him. He was to be a gentleman, virtually a non-drinker who patronised coffee shops.'[1]

Though the brothers had been close, Peter felt that the pressure of the case and the advice of Patrick's acquaintances had caused a rift: 'I was to be demonised. I was the one with the extravagant character … I was transformed from being his intimate friend and advisor into being his servant, almost his slave.'[2]

Sir John Esmonde, Thomas Connolly and Niall McCarthy instructed by James O'Connor and Son, appeared for Kavanagh. John A. Costello, James MacMahon and William Finlay instructed by McCann, White and Fitzgerald appeared for *The Leader* while William O'Brien Fitzgerald, Brian Walsh and Fergus Flood instructed by Brannigan and Matthews represented the printers, Argus. Given the number of lawyers on show, the issue of costs at the end of the trial would be crucial. Mr Justice Teevan was selected to preside. It was his first case as a High Court judge. He had taken his seat for the first time on the Bench in the High Court just the day before.[3]

John Aloysius Costello appeared for the defence. He was a celebrity in his own right, even better known in Ireland at the time than Kavanagh. Born in Dublin in 1891, Costello had been educated in O'Connell Schools by the Christian Brothers where, as he put it himself, he was well versed in the 'four Rs: Reading, Riting, Rithmetic and Rebellion'.[4] At University College Dublin he had studied history, languages and literature, obtaining his BA degree in 1911. A brilliant student, he won a number of scholarships and prizes. He obtained his Bachelor of Laws degree in 1914 and was called to the bar in 1925.

In 1926 Costello was appointed Attorney General, a position he held until 1932. First elected to Dáil Éireann in 1933 for the constituency of County Dublin, he subsequently represented the Dublin South-East constituency, which ironically covered the Pembroke Road area, so Kavanagh was one of his constituents. Though his close friends called him Jack, he was generally known as John A. Costello.

In February 1948 Costello was elected Taoiseach of the first Inter-Party Government, which was made up of Fine Gael, Labour, Clann na Talmhan, Clann na Poblachta, National Labour and Independents. The coalition remained in power from 1948 to 1951 and Costello is best remembered for the Repeal of the External Relations Act and the formal declaration of the Republic on Easter Monday 1949. After the defeat of the coalition in the general election of 1951, Costello had returned to his legal practice. It was the opinion of the Kavanaghs that Costello was a publicity seeker who was missing the limelight and that was why he took on this high-profile case. As Jack White in the *Spectator* put it: 'For the legal eagles an extra grain of piquancy was added for the hearing by the fact that the judge and the leading counsel of the defence were prominent members of opposed political parties. Mr Justice Teevan was Attorney General in Mr de Valera's government, availing himself of the privilege of that position, he moved to the High Court when a vacancy occurred …'[5] Not only that, Sir John Esmonde, senior counsel for Kavanagh had also been an active member of Costello's party.

Anthony Cronin characterised Costello as 'a forceful, occasional rather savage lawyer of the old school …'[6] A political commentator of the time described Costello as 'impressive, with a resonant and slightly Dublin accent, of sturdy build and with a rough charm … he has none of the charisma of a Pearse, a Griffith or a de Valera …'[7]

'The Irishman's Diary' in *The Irish Times* on 9 February 1954 reported the following: 'Mr Costello wore what must be his most venerable wig, so yellowed with age that it looked almost ginger in some lights. The plaintiff favoured a navy-blue, Burberry-type coat with a check-shirt, a sober dark tie and a coiffure in which the hair was brushed forward from the south-west base of the skull into a Napoleonic forelock which slanted over his left eyebrow.'[8]

It remained to be seen how this pugnacious style of his would fare up against the articulate Mr Kavanagh.

Sir John Esmonde had been elected as Irish Parliamentary Party MP for North Tipperary while serving in the First World War with the Leinster Regiment. He chose not to defend his seat in the 1918 general election. He subsequently served as a Fine Gael TD for Wexford from 1937 to 1944, but lost his Dáil seat in the 1944 general election. He became a barrister at the King's Inns, Dublin, and was called to the inner bar as senior counsel in 1942 and bencher in 1948. He was re-elected TD for Fine Gael from 1948 to 1951. In 1948 he was suggested as a possible Taoiseach by Seán MacBride, on the grounds that he had no link to either side in the Civil War. It was one of the ironies of the case that he faced John A. Costello, who was elected as Taoiseach in 1948, in the Kavanagh trial. Esmonde retired from politics before the 1951 general election, when he resigned his constituency.

In his statement of claim Mr Kavanagh said that in the course of his profession as a writer and journalist he had published numerous works and had contributed articles to well-known literary periodicals and journals including the

Spectator, the *Manchester Guardian*, the *Observer* and *Time and Tide*, and had broadcast on literary topics from Radio Éireann and the BBC. It was also noted that he had written material for the *Encyclopaedia Americana*.

The entire article from *The Leader* was read into record for the benefit of the jury who got to hear for the first time about the poet, hunkered on a bar-stool with a voice like a load of gravel sliding down the side of a quarry, telling the sylph-like redheads and dewy-eyed brunettes clustered around him that '*Yous have no merit, no merit at all*'. It was an account they were to become all too familiar with.

In the statement of claim, it was alleged that 'by the said words and by the said article as a whole the plaintiff had been held up to odium, hatred, ridicule and contempt, and had been gravely damaged in his reputation and in his said profession'.

Furthermore, the article represented Kavanagh as 'a person of vicious dissolute and intemperate habits, that he is a sponger, that he is opprobrious and unjustifiably abusive in his dealings with others, and he possesses only an inadequate acquaintance with the grammar and syntax of the English language'. The article held him out to be 'a person of very limited mental ability and lacks reasoning power, and that as a writer and in his private capacity he displays vanity, shallowness and cunning and is not to be taken seriously', and 'that the plaintiff is of unbalanced disposition, a snob and ashamed of his origin' and that 'he is entirely ignorant and incapable of writing seriously about urban or city life'. It went on to say that 'the plaintiff had started *Kavanagh's Weekly* with family finance out of malice and hatred towards certain periodicals, newspapers and literary agencies because of their refusal or neglect to employ him', and that '*Kavanagh's Weekly* was a childish publication, not to be taken seriously' that had been 'started from motives of personal vanity and spite and not in fact with a *bona fide* literary intent'.

Kavanagh had been 'gravely injured in his character, credit and reputation, and in his profession as a writer and journalist, and he has been brought into public hatred, scandal and contempt'.

The plaintiff claimed:

1. Damages
2. An injunction to restrain the Defendants ... from further printing, publishing or circulating ... the said or any similar defamatory statements.[9]

The two defendants, *The Leader* and Argus, put forward a virtually identical defence. They denied that the words complained of in the profile were printed or published falsely or maliciously, with any of the meanings alleged, with any defamatory meaning or that they were capable of bearing any such meaning.[10] They claimed that the words were fair and *bona fide* comment made without malice upon a matter of public interest and that in so far as the words consisted of allegations of fact, they were true in substance and in fact, and were fair comments made in good faith and without malice upon those facts.[11]

Sir John Esmonde opened the case for the plaintiff. He stated that Mr Kavanagh appeared before the court as 'a rising if not a risen Irishman of letters ...' The article in *The*

Leader not only attacked him in his professional capacity but in his private capacity. His client, he asserted, led 'a quiet life of early-to-bed and early rising' and 'his principal recreation was racing which would appear to everyone in the country'.[12] Mr Kavanagh did not want to be held up as 'a buffoon and be lampooned as he was in the article'.[13]

Sir John told the court that a very reasonable request was made to the defendants for the name of the author of the profile but it was not disclosed. It was a fair assumption to make that the writer of the article knew Mr Kavanagh and that the author wrote with venom against him. He stumbled over the pronunciation of the word 'gurrier' used in the profile, saying: 'I take it that is the proper way to pronounce that word. It is the first time I have seen it.'

'It is in Mr Kavanagh's writings,' defence counsel John A. Costello informed the court.

Mr Connolly took exception to his intervention: 'I know *The Leader* is bursting to get going but there will be plenty of opportunity later.'

'I am sorry, I could not resist it,' Costello said.

The court adjourned without counsel finishing his opening statement.

'MY EARLY-TO-BED, EARLY-TO-RISE CLIENT'

The next day when the case resumed before Justice Teevan it was obvious that it had caught the public's attention. Every available seat was taken and there were 100 people crammed into the standing space. The courtroom was so crowded that counsel and journalists had difficulty in reaching their seats in the afternoon. Peter and Patrick Kavanagh exchanged handwritten notes during the proceedings. Peter advised his brother to relax and to 'keep still if it kills you'.[14]

Sir John Esmonde continued with his opening statement, outlining the correspondence between the plaintiff's solicitors and the defendants. He told the jury it would not be necessary for them to go as far as searching for innuendoes in the article complained of because, if there ever was plain speaking, it was in that document.[15]

The Leader still refused to divulge the name of the author of the profile prompting Esmonde to say: 'Perhaps this unknown cloak-and-dagger man may have the temerity to get up here in this court and bear out one of the defences in the file here, that it is legitimate criticism. We don't know who he is and his name has never been mentioned. Is he in Ireland? Is he in Dublin? Is he in this court?'[16]

The defendants, according to Sir John, had pleaded the defence of 'fair comment' and also a 'rolled-up plea' – that insofar as these matters were statements of fact, they were also true – 'that my early-to-bed, early-to-rise client was seen in some public house under circumstances as described in this filthy first paragraph of the article.' In Esmonde's opinion, the beginning of that profile was:

… a complete example of ridicule. Can you envisage our unknown cloak-and-dagger author metaphorically patting himself on the back at inventing these scurrilous words to use against Mr Kavanagh? Can you imagine the satisfaction that venomous man can have who is afraid to come forward? A critic must not go out of his way to attack the private character of an author. In this article you will find here and there – dispersed as out of a pepper-pot – attacks on the private character of the author.

Esmonde concluded that given that the defendants were standing over the allegations in the article and had made no attempt to apologise, if the jury found in Mr Kavanagh's favour they should take this into account when assessing damages.

The defence of 'fair comment' in its legal sense:

> … confers protection against liability for those who make defamatory statements which contain fair comments on matters of public interest. The burden of raising this defence rests on the defendant. He must establish a number of proofs. He must show that the statement consisted of comment and of facts supporting the comment, and, if the facts are not included in the statement, they must at least be discernible from it. The supporting facts must be shown to be true, and the comment must be shown to be fair in the sense that there is some logical connection between the facts and the comment. Fairness thus has a different connotation to its ordinary usage. The subject matter of the communication must be shown to have been a matter of public interest.[17]

Patrick Kavanagh took the stand. In answer to some gentle probing by his own senior counsel, Thomas Connolly, he was taken through his early life and literary career. Eventually Costello lost patience with the pace of the questioning: 'Could we have when he left Monaghan?' he interrupted.

A brochure published by the Department of External Affairs called 'Introducing Ireland' that referred to Kavanagh's work under literature was produced. It stated that the 'most important living poet, however, is Patrick Kavanagh whose language in "The Great Hunger" and certain of his earlier poems has the unmistakable mark of genius'. Costello objected to this being presented as evidence on the grounds that it was irrelevant and that they did not know who had written it or the value of its contents. He claimed: 'I could bring up forty people to say he is a bad poet, but I am not going to do it. It is quite irrelevant what other people think of him.'

Shortly afterwards the case was adjourned for lunch.

When the case resumed in the afternoon Mr Costello complained that he could not hear what the witness was saying. 'Would you speak up, please?' Mr Connolly asked his client and reminded him (and the jury), 'you know the article says you have a voice reminiscent of a load of gravel sliding down the side of a quarry'.[18]

'He does not want to let the jury see that it does,' Costello commented.

Connolly then took Patrick through some parts of the offending article. Asked if he had met the Lady Cunard referred to in the article, Kavanagh replied: 'I have not. I never even travelled in one of her ships.'

When Connolly inquired about the inspiration for *Kavanagh's Weekly* Patrick stated that it was love of country that had motivated him. Asked how his objectives to earn his living in Ireland as a journalist, poet, novelist and broadcaster had been affected by the article, Kavanagh said that it was so totally the opposite of what he was that it was an attempt to create another 'him' that did not exist at all.

'There is a statement in the article that your talents had been diverted into unsuitable channels,' Connolly said. 'Do you agree that your talents were affected in any way?'

'No, I flatly disagree with it.' Kavanagh went on to say that the profile represented him as a clown, a fool or a buffoon. He concluded by asserting: 'My argument has been that literature is not the activity of wild bohemians but is part of the religious mind. That it is, in fact part of religion. All that gloomy and wild life we hear about is anathema to me.'

After the comparatively easy ride given him by his own counsel, Kavanagh now faced a more trying ordeal and a wily opponent, ex-Taoiseach John A. Costello. As *The Irish Times* put it: 'His cross-examination by John A. Costello alternately had the court in bouts of laughter and contrasting sharp silences'.[19] Costello began his cross-examination with the question: 'I suppose it was because of your religious attitude that your book [*Tarry Flynn*] was banned by the censor for three days?'

'I don't know.'

'… and portion of "The Great Hunger" was banned because of its obscenity?'

'Portion of it was banned. I don't know why.'

Costello went on to ask Kavanagh if he knew that 'if you do anything contrary to the Censorship Act you thereby threaten yourself with imprisonment?'

'You are telling me that,' said Kavanagh.

'I will tell you more about it later on,' Costello added, to widespread laughter in the court.

Costello then went on to request the plaintiff to define the word 'gurrier' and was told that it was a euphemism for the 'gutter'. (The word had been used in the second paragraph of the profile: 'the self-preserving instinct of the country-boy thrown among the rough crowd of city gurriers whose only thought is to do him down …')

'It is part of your verbal currency?' Costello asked.

'It is not. It is common currency in Dublin.'

Costello made the point: 'It appears, at all events, that the word "gurrier" that appears in this article was taken from your works?'

'I do not agree.'

'Isn't it quoted in this article?'

'What about it?'

More laughter in the court.

Costello: 'We will see about it later on. If it comes from the word gutter, what does it mean?'

Kavanagh: 'That would be a long story to go into, the meaning of words.'

C: 'It has a very subtle shade of meaning?'

K: 'I would not think that it would have.'

C: 'Is this not a derogatory word?'

K: 'It is not a friendly word, I will say.'

C: 'Come on now, isn't it a very derogatory word with a very deep Dublin shade of meaning to it?'

K: 'Oh, good God no, there is no dirty meaning to it.'

C: 'I didn't say it had a dirty meaning: I said a Dublin meaning.'

(Laughter)

K: 'I don't know.'

C: 'You don't know Dublin very well and you don't care very much for Dublin.'

'Is that a question?' Mr Connolly for the plaintiff intervened.

'It is not Mr Costello,' Justice Teevan decreed.

'Do you tell the judge that you don't know the shade of meaning of the word "gurrier"?' Costello asked one more time.

'I don't,' Kavanagh replied.[20]

A discussion on grammar and spelling ensued. Kavanagh stated that 'anything that was clear was good grammar … If you speak good grammar, you will be clear and it is a rarity to hear it.'

'That is a very useful observation,' Costello agreed, 'do you stick to that?'

K: 'It must be good grammar to be clear.'

C: 'You are sticking to that?'

K: 'I'll stick to the truth.'

C: 'Do you stick to that?'

K: 'I'll stick to the truth.'

C: 'I assume that when you said that anything that is clear is good grammar –'

K: 'That is a short definition. You could not explain the whole English language in one phrase.'

C: 'May the Lord preserve us from your explanations!'

'That is not fair on the witness, Mr Costello,' Mr Justice Teevan intervened, 'I do not think you should make an observation like that.'

'That is not fair,' Kavanagh said, 'you will allow me to continue. I will explain more about the English language if you give me more time, but I cannot do so if you keep shouting at me.'

'Anything that is clear is good grammar?'

'Yes, and anything that is good grammar is clear. If you will speak good grammar you will be very clear.'

(Laughter)

'That may be so.'[21]

(More laughter)

Mr Justice Teevan said to Kavanagh: 'In the innuendoes it is said that you have an inadequate acquaintance with the grammar and syntax of the English language.'

Kavanagh took umbrage: 'I am master of the thing. That is a most atrocious thing to say.'

Next up from Costello was a request for a definition of the word 'wan'. Kavanagh replied: 'It was one of those things used to make a point, to achieve a mood. It is written in an element of drollery and don't forget, the element of drollery is a very powerful thing.'

Mr Costello pressed him on the point: 'Are you trying to suggest that I don't know how to spell the word "one"?'

'I am not trying to do anything of the sort. I am suggesting you did use the word.'

'Many times.'

Continuing down the lexicographical path, Costello asked him to define 'bucklep' and 'bucklepper'. Kavanagh stated that he had defined it for the past three years everywhere and asked if he had to do it again. Mr Justice told him he must define it again. Kavanagh replied that he used these words to describe a school of writers who put forward as a typical Irishman a man who was a rolling, lepping, drinking semi-tinker type.[22] 'You see them everywhere in plays,' he said, 'this enormous monstrosity has been established and it is not a sincere thing at all … That is what I call bucklepping. He is always going through the streets and tearing his hair.'

'If it isn't slang, would you agree it is colloquial?' asked Costello.

'No, it is an invented word.'

'By who?'

'It was invented by me.'

'You may have invented the particular very rambling meaning but we all know the word.'

'That is what I mean by it,' Kavanagh insisted. 'I have very clearly stated what I mean.'

'THE FIRBOLG FELLOWS HAD BIG BELLIES'

Asked to define the word 'Firbolg', Kavanagh said: 'I suppose you would have to go to somebody in the museum or an archaeologist.'

C: 'You used that term about other people.'

K: 'It is one of the ancient races of Ireland.'

C: 'Didn't you use it in a derogatory sense?'

K: 'I'm not denying that the Firbolgs were supposed to be a rather inferior race.'

C: 'The Firbolg fellows had big bellies.'

K: 'I do not know about that.'

C: 'You used the term without knowing what it means.'

K: 'You would have to run over the context to tell. I know the meaning of a lot of words.'

C: 'You used that word as a colloquial slang term in a derogatory sense.'

K: 'You would have to read the context.'

C: 'Will you define "bogman"? What does that mean?'

K: 'He is a character generally speaking in a novel of an Irishman generally who is guilty of murder, infanticide and any other crimes that are possible. Bogmen is part of novels. It is the same thing as "bucklepper". It is part of the school.'

Costello moved on to *The Green Fool*: 'It cost your publishers £100 in a libel action.' Kavanagh argued that it was different to this case because *The Green Fool* was a work of fiction.

Costello asked about a phrase 'Divil a' that', which had been used in *The Green Fool*.

'That is fiction,' Kavanagh insisted.

'But it is language,' Costello responded.

Costello did not stop there but went on to discuss Sir John Esmonde's opening remarks, stating: 'You are a simple man, early-to-bed, early-to-rise, who only wants a quiet life?'

'Very simple. I want a quiet life,' Kavanagh replied.

C: 'I suppose there will be many a chuckle among the intelligentsia when they hear the description of your counsel that you are a simple, quiet, unassuming, early-to-bed man who only wants to be considered seriously to earn his living. There will be many a chuckle at that in your circles.'

K: 'I disagree with you.'

C: 'Do you accept that description of yourself, to go to his Lordship and the jury?'

K: 'I do.'

'No bucklepper, no Firbolg?' Costello prodded away.

K: 'I am not claiming to be a saint. I am only claiming that I do my best.'

C: 'We say you are the greatest living poet.'

K: 'That doesn't butter much parsnips.'

C: 'You would accept that description.'

K: 'I am now.'

C: 'With a serious message?'

K: 'I assure you I am serious about it. It is more important to me than anything in the world.'

With regard to *The Leader*, Kavanagh was asked if he was familiar of it. He said he was not.

C: 'It is the only newspaper that has lasted for over half a century in this country.'

K: 'I do not know much about it.'

C: 'Are we to take it you do not read *The Leader* unless it has a profile in it?'

K: 'I read it an odd time.'

As to its political stance Kavanagh stated: 'I know it was offensive towards many distinguished Irishmen.'

Costello began to say: 'Do you know that a Cardinal has given his view that –' Connolly for the plaintiff attempted to object but Costello continued: 'Do you disagree with Cardinal D'Alton and Lennox Robinson and other people?' (D'Alton and Robinson had contributed complimentary letters to *The Leader*'s Jubilee edition in 1950.) Following another objection,

Costello said that he was merely highlighting the point that *The Leader* was a paper of importance and influence in the life of the country. Under further questioning Kavanagh asserted that at one time *The Leader* may have been influential under its founder D.P. Moran, but it had not been for the last twenty years.

Costello went on to question Kavanagh on various controversies his work had stirred up: 'You have had books suppressed for obscenity?'

'Portions,' replied Kavanagh.

'Was not a portion of "The Great Hunger" suppressed for indecency?'

'I have no knowledge of it,' said Kavanagh.

'Nonsense,' replied Costello.

Kavanagh disagreed, stating that parts of 'The Great Hunger' were deleted on the grounds of art, not on the grounds of morality: 'It was rather naïve and not interesting enough. I threw it out.'

'The police came to you and told you it was obscene?'

'Practically all the obscene bits are still in,' Kavanagh maintained, to the accompaniment of much laughter in the crowded court. After a pause Kavanagh himself joined in with it.

C: 'Practically? All the obscene parts are practically in? Were some of the obscene parts out? There were some obscene parts omitted?'

K: 'Parts were omitted.'

C: 'Obscene parts?'

K: 'Yes. And other parts.'

As regards a visit by the authorities to interview him, Kavanagh was evasive.

C: 'Were there two police officers?'

K: 'In civilian clothes.'

C: 'Stop fencing. Were there two police officers?'

Justice Teevan intervened: 'Answer the question Mr Kavanagh.'

K: 'Technically, I believe they were.'

C: 'Don't you know very well?'

K: 'I know I believed it.'

C: 'Didn't they tell you?'

K: 'They did.'

C: 'But you said, "technically".'

Costello mentioned a review of 'The Great Hunger' by Robert Greacen, which had stated that it 'was a blast of defiance flung at the censors'.

'I cannot help what is written,' Kavanagh said in reply to the accusation. After further debate Justice Teevan again intervened: 'Were you threatened with proceedings?'

'They asked me my views. We had a talk about Chaucer. They didn't know much about him.'

'Do you agree there were obscene portions in it?' Teevan asked.

'Not for the really adult.'

'Did the police officers say that proceedings would be brought against you?'

'They did not say that. We had a confab or talk. They showed me the thing and asked "did you write that?" I said, "yes", and they said "all right".'

Kavanagh pointed out that he had liked the two guards who had come to see him.

'We were very friendly,' he told the court, 'we parted in a haze of goodwill.'

'Is that "haze of goodwill" any relation of the Celtic Twilight, by any chance?' Costello asked.

Kavanagh replied: 'It is not.'

Costello returned to the attack: 'Did you sign a statement?'

'No, they didn't ask me,' Kavanagh stated, 'you are wrong about me. I'll try to defend my own point of view and I'll try to get it home in spite of you.'

Mr Justice Teevan intervened to ask when Costello thought he would be finished with the witness. 'I have only just begun. I am only skirmishing yet,' Costello replied.

Costello moved on to an article in *The Bell*, which John Ryan had written, in an issue to which Kavanagh had contributed a poem.

K: 'He is an acquaintance of mine – he is a friend, I suppose he is.'

C: 'You will not admit he is a friend?'

K: 'Of course he is a friend of mine. There is no use getting into that detail.'

Kavanagh denied that he read the magazine, only his own part in it: 'The general rule of journalism is, if you have anything by yourself printed you ignore everything else except what you wrote yourself. No man reads anything but his own stories.'

After further examination he continued: 'As a matter of fact, I cut my poem out so that I would not see the rest of it.' Kavanagh joined in the general laughter.

Costello quoted from the article in which John Ryan had referred to 'The Great Hunger' as 'the most important poetical work to come from Ireland in our generation', but no sooner had it been published than 'special police agents descended on the man and subjected him to an unceasing interrogation for many days'.

Costello went on to allege that anyone reading the article would assume that allegations of obscenity were true. Kavanagh argued that a reader might believe that there was some 'legend' about the matter.

The judge asked him to expand on this. He explained that a reader might assume there was some rumour about the matter. The writer of the article was saying, in effect: 'Why do you kick the man to death?'

Costello asked Kavanagh why he had not contradicted the article if the allegations were not true. And now he was complaining about the same information appearing in *The Leader*.

'That is because it is not true,' Kavanagh maintained.

Anthony Cronin characterised Costello's stance as pretending, 'if that were possible, to be more ignorant of art and letters than the jury themselves, while concealing behind his pretended bafflement a mind as sharp as a knife'.[23]

It would seem that the defence's intention in asking Kavanagh about his language was to imply that the words used in the profile were similar to those used by Kavanagh himself in his own work and that much of that work was itself controversial. Costello's strategy was to attack Kavanagh as if he was the defendant and not the other way around. It could also be said that Kavanagh's team should perhaps have been more alert and protective of their client in the witness box. Costello's pugnacity had rattled him.

The session finished with Kavanagh still under cross-examination. The case was adjourned until the following Monday. Kavanagh would have the weekend to contemplate his circumstances. It was obvious that the defence's approach was to focus on him. They were going to scrutinise all his writings. Once it was accepted that all of Kavanagh's writings were fair game, Costello would have enormous scope.

By the end of the first few days of the trial, Kavanagh looked as if he could do with the break. His ordeal was only just beginning.

Chapter 12

'Nothing is complimentary that takes away a man's dinner'

A queue extending halfway around the circular Main Hall of the Four Courts building waited for nearly an hour to be allowed into the public seats of the Court. A policeman at the door checked all entering. Many did not find a place either to sit or stand, even when a great number of jurors for other cases had left the Court …When the jury for the case was called, three members could not be found at first. They were later discovered to be in the Main Hall and were summoned from there to the jury-box.[1]

The cross-examination of Kavanagh resumed with Costello asking him: 'I think you did admit in your direct examination that the Minister for External Affairs [Frank Aiken] had refused to pay your passage to the United States to enable you to deliver a series of lectures there, or did you?'

'Pardon?'

'Did you or did you not do that?'

'I admit I got no notification that it was refused except what I saw in the papers.'

THE IRISH TIMES, TUESDAY, FEBRUARY 9, 1954

FURTHER CROSS-EXAMINATION OF NOVELIST IN LIBEL ACTION

"That monstrous paragraph"

Mr. Patrick Kavanagh all day in witness-box

The Irish Times devoted page after page to the trial. It was treated as a social as well as a legal event.

'That is not the question. I understood, perhaps incorrectly, that it was your suggestion that the statement in this article about this matter was incorrect. Do you remember the statement?'

'I remember, I believe quite well, that the Minister did veto it, the unanimous decision of the Cultural Relations Committee, which he was perfectly entitled to do.'

'I want to clear this up for once and for all,' Costello declared, 'I and my colleagues thought you and your colleagues were throwing doubt on it. The phrase is perfectly clear. "The Minister for External Affairs last year refused to pay his passage to the United States to enable him to deliver a series of lectures there." Is that or is that not a correct statement of fact?'

'It is a twisted and perverted statement of fact. It is as much as if I went to the Minister to get £100 off him,' replied Kavanagh.

'That is not stated at all and we never heard that suggestion until you made it now.'

'But it is implied. It is the main implication in that.'

'This matter received considerable publicity at the time …'

'I am aware of that.'

'Was there a letter written by your friend John Ryan, who had been then editor of *Envoy* on 20 September 1951 headed "Minister refuses to grant poet's lecture tour expenses" [this in fact, was the headline *The Irish Times* used for their report on the controversy]. Would you look at that?' Costello gave a copy of *The Irish Times* article to Kavanagh.

Sir John Esmonde objected on behalf of his client: 'I do not want to intervene too often but a document has been handed up to the witness. I would like to know what purpose is behind this question. Is it as to credibility or proof of the existence of a fact in the impugned article? If the truth of the statement is challenged there is a way of proving that.'

Mr Costello replied that it was a letter from Mr Ryan drawing attention to the incident. He was of the opinion that he could cross-examine the witness on the matter: 'If there is any question about it I could ask the Minister for External Affairs to come down here.' He wanted to prove that the statement had been made in public.

Justice Teevan ruled that the newspaper should not be put into evidence, just the question of whether the statement had been made in public.

'With great respect,' Costello said, 'I want it to go in. Otherwise I would be giving secondary evidence by asking him did he see the letter.'

'I do not want to be too much of a nuisance …' Sir John Esmonde said, showing a rather relaxed attitude compared to the belligerence of his opposing counsel.

At the end of the legal arguments Justice Teevan decided:

'We will take it as we go along … We will take it piece by piece.'

Costello asked the witness if he knew that his friend Mr Ryan had published the letter referred to.

Kavanagh replied: 'In *this* case I do not know the author of the article.'

C: 'It doesn't matter whether you do or not. Answer the question.'

K: 'I will answer it by saying in a case of this kind the mood in which the letter is written and the intention is very important.'

C: 'I only want the fact for the jury.'

K: 'Well, and what is more important than fact is truth. That kind of sensational journalism is not to be taken seriously.'

C: 'Did you know that letter was written by your friend John Ryan?'

K: 'Yes, I saw that letter.'

C: 'Protesting against the action of the Minister for External Affairs in refusing to pay your passage to the United States of America to enable you to deliver a series of lectures?'

K: 'I know nothing about it except what I saw in the paper.'

Kavanagh went on to state: 'I am not responsible for Mr Ryan and I do not stand over what he wrote.'

Having made his point, Costello finally moved on. He asked the witness if he had read the profile of which he had complained.

'I looked through it … I can tell you I read it with horror,' Kavanagh responded, amidst laughter in the court.

'I did not ask you that. Please answer the question, a very simple one. How many times did you read the article?'

K: 'It would be impossible to tell.'

C: 'How many times did you read that article before you went to see your solicitor?'

K: 'I read it only once and only in glances of horror if I may say so.'

At this stage the cross-examination was punctuated by bursts of laughter from the gallery.

'You may say so,' Costello replied. 'You read it once then you trotted off to your solicitor with peremptory instructions to issue proceedings for libel?'

K: 'I was scarcely fit to write a letter to a solicitor for a week on account of it.'

C: 'Because you were indignant?'

K: 'I was not indignant; I was horror-stricken, I was wounded, my Lord and those who knew me and saw me at the time knew that.'

C: 'You say from one reading of that article you were able to draw that conclusion.'

K: 'They were there and they were drawn.'

Costello and Kavanagh went on to discuss the first sentence of the profile, 'a pard-like spirit, beautiful and swift' (a direct quotation from Shelley's 'Adonais: An Elegy on the Death of John Keats'). 'I suppose you will agree that this is one of the most famous verses in English literature?' Costello suggested.

'No,' said Kavanagh.

Laughter followed until Justice Teevan intervened, asking for silence and warning the public that 'there must be some limit to the interference by way of reaction from the public in the court'.

'Do you agree,' Costello resumed, 'that these lines were written by one of the greatest lyric poets of the English language and perhaps in any language about another lyric poet, also one of the greatest in the English language, and perhaps, in any language?'

K: 'I will agree it is written about a great lyric poet.'

C: 'You have expressed your admiration for Keats as a poet?'

K: 'Yes, I think he is very good.'

C: 'You don't much care for Shelley?'

K: 'I would have to sit down and write on this to be precise.'

C: 'You will agree Shelley is regarded fairly extensively as a very good poet?'

K: 'He is not.'

C: 'Not what?'

K: 'Not among the greatest.'

C: 'Is he a great poet?'

K: 'I doubt it.'

C: 'Well at all events he has written verse well known to anybody who knows anything about literature about a great man whom you regard as a great poet. For the benefit of those who do not know what a pard is, will you agree it is a leopard?'

K: 'It might be.'

C: 'It is used in Shakespeare also, "full of strange oaths and bearded like the pard", I think it is.'

K: 'Quite true.'

C: 'What do you regard the phrase "pard-like spirit" as meaning?'

K: 'It means very little.'

C: 'Is it a highly complimentary phrase?'

K: 'I suppose it is.'

C: 'You are making an admission very grudgingly.'

K: 'I like to make a considered judgment when talking about a serious subject.'

C: 'At all events it is the image of the leopard, beautiful and swift, and that image, I suggest of poetic vision and merit, is what Shelley said on the death of Keats. Do you agree about that?'

K: 'That is a very diffuse kind of question.'

C: 'At any rate he has written a verse which is well known about a man whom you regard as a great poet?'

Kavanagh, at long last, agreed.

Costello continued: 'Does it require a serious judgment to say that the verse by Shelley about Keats is highly complimentary, a highly complimentary description of a poet?'

Kavanagh refused to be pinned down: 'It is very hard to say what it is at the moment.'

Costello quoted a longer excerpt from 'Adonais':

A pard-like spirit, beautiful and swift,
A love in desolation masked – a power
Girt around with weakness – it can scarce uplift
The weight of the super-incumbent hour

It is a dying lamp, a falling shower
A breaking billow …

Costello asked if those were complimentary phrases.

'I don't know what you want me to say, but I will say what I think,' Kavanagh replied. 'It is rhetoric and rings false. That is what I would give if I was writing an essay on it.'

Costello argued: 'I think you are clever enough to anticipate what I am going to say, that the phrase "a pard-like beautiful spirit" is the theme and thesis of this article, and that it is applicable to you notwithstanding the other things that may have been said in the article?'

Kavanagh disagreed saying: 'It is much more like the Edinburgh review of Keats which told him to go back to his pills.' (Keats had studied to become a surgeon's apprentice in an apothecary shop.)

Costello pressed on: 'This article, having taken this phrase as its theme, comes to the conclusion, in addition, that, notwithstanding the external matters mentioned about you, you are "our finest living poet"?'

K: 'I do not follow the question.'

C: 'I think you are cleverer than me and that you know what I mean.'

Sir John Esmonde intervened on Kavanagh's behalf and said that it was two questions in one.

C: 'I will reduce the question to words of one syllable for the poet, if necessary. Do you agree that the phrase "pard-like spirit, beautiful and swift" is a complimentary phrase?'

K: 'I do not think it would get you a job.'

C: 'That is not the point.'

K: 'That is the key-note of modern living.'

C: 'Do you agree that it is complimentary?'

K: 'Yes, with a strong note of starvation implicit in it.'

C: 'That may be the fate of poets. But do you agree it is a complimentary phrase?'

K: 'Nothing is a complimentary phrase that takes away a man's dinner.'

When asked if the phrase was applicable to him as a poet, Kavanagh replied that he did not wish to have his poetic life separated from his life as a man: 'The man comes first. That is the most important thing.'

C: 'That is not an answer.'

K: 'It is impossible to separate what might be called the poetic man from the ordinary man. You cannot do that.'

Costello asked, did not the writer of the profile come to the conclusion that Kavanagh was our finest living poet?

'I would prefer he did not. In saying so he is unmannerly,' Kavanagh replied. 'Is he saying the finest living poet in Ireland or the world, or where? I will have to go through it and see.' He went on to call it 'a left-handed compliment'.

C: 'It is a left-handed compliment for you to be described as our finest living poet?'

K: 'Dozens of people have said that before. It doesn't put any butter on your bread.'

C: 'Does it bring people who said it to libel actions in court?'

K: 'That is what I mean. They had to say all the foul things about me in the rest of the article to build me up to this later, where they could slander me on my livelihood.'

Costello referred to the profile and its assertion that 'The Great Hunger' was probably the best poem published in Ireland since Goldsmith's 'The Deserted Village'. Esmonde intervened to point out that this was meant to be a cross-examination of the witness and not an address to the jury: 'My friend is a leader of the Bar and knows that.'

'HELLO SHAKESPEARE'

'You said that the author of this profile built you up by the expressions to which I referred in order to denigrate you by other expressions?' asked Costello.

Kavanagh replied: 'There are various grades of sneering at a man. One of the ways is that I have been sneered at in public by people who did not like me. I remember once people calling me "Will Shakespeare". That is an insult, because it is not true. Ignorant people say that kind of thing all the time. They build you up and make you look outrageous. People have saluted me by saying "Hello Shakespeare". That is an insult. They compare me to Shakespeare.'

Justice Teevan intervened to sum up Costello's line of questioning: 'Do you agree that the purpose of the article and the conclusion the writer reaches is to show that you are our finest poet?'

'No,' Kavanagh remained adamant.

As to Mr Kavanagh's activity as a critic himself, Mr Costello asked him: 'Have you not attacked pretty well nearly every Irish writer of contemporary times?'

K: 'I have attacked the writing but never the writer.'

C: 'I accept the correction.'

K: 'I never intruded on the sacred personality of any man.'

C: 'You were very destructive in your criticisms.'

K: 'A lover is often very destructive.'

C: 'Do you agree that you were?'

K: 'No.'

C: 'Are you content to have your own standards of criticism, that you applied to others, applied to your own works?'

K: 'I think that anyone who takes a stand on the real Olympian heights says: "you can say what you like about me".'

'About your work?' Mr Justice Teevan asked.

Kavanagh replied: 'Yes. I have never been worried about criticism. In fact I am myself far more self-critical than anyone that ever wrote about me was.'

'Explain what you mean by that,' Costello said, 'because I did not understand it.'

Kavanagh went on to explain that his standards of criticism were universal standards, used throughout the world.

Costello then quoted an article by Kavanagh from *Envoy:* 'Comparative criticism is criticism without standards. A true creative critic is a sweeping critic who violently hates certain things because they are weeds which choke the field against the crop which he wants to sow. Truth is personality, and no genuine writer, as a critic, was ever anything but absolute in his destructiveness. If a piece of writing is good there is nothing one can or should say except the words, 'it is good'. If it is bad there is not much necessity to say anything either as time will do the job of destruction. The comparative critic is a parasite who is constantly looking around him, waiting for the appearance of a new writer who will add to the dwindling supply of names that make literary news.'

Kavanagh stated that he agreed thoroughly with himself: 'I stand over all that. That is perfectly all right. It is simple Christianity.'

The sentiments in the passage were his point of view. It was the Olympian standard and it was not destructive: 'The motive behind it is an attempt to try to establish true standards and I will quote Blake, "a Last Judgment is necessary because fools flourish".'

C: 'You quoted that in *Envoy*.'

K: 'Yes.'

C: 'You said in *Envoy* that comparative criticism is criticism without standards?'

K: 'That is correct.'

C: 'You have just said that you must have standards?'

K: 'Comparative criticism is comparing the bad with the less bad.'

Kavanagh went on to explain that he and a few others attempted to establish a true judgment in Ireland, a metropolitan judgment.

Costello said: 'And that consisted of attacking everybody.'

'That is an observation,' Justice Teevan pointed out to Costello, 'it is denigrating – it is an attack on the witness.'

'The result of that standard was that you attacked every living Irish poet,' Costello rephrased.

'Do you mean attacked personally,' Justice Teevan asked, 'or their works?'

'In his works,' Costello clarified.

'It was essential to establish that standard,' Kavanagh insisted.

'Do you agree that you did attack the works of every living poet in Ireland?' the judge repeated.

'May I suggest,' Mr Costello offered, 'the words "every contemporary poet" instead of "every living poet"?'

Patrick Kavanagh came up with his own modification: 'I would like to correct that and say "every contemporary versifier".'

'That underlines my point,' Costello claimed, 'that all those people who thought they were poets were, in your view, versifiers.'

'They are versifiers too,' Kavanagh said, 'but that is a moot point.'

'Do you agree,' Costello continued, 'that in your criticism you attacked the works of nearly all the contemporary Irish poets ... or versifiers?'

'I must say that it was absolutely essential to our purpose to clear the way for a new idea. It is nothing to what they did in every other country,' replied Kavanagh.

C: 'Does that mean that you did?'

K: 'We were not interested in destroying them. We were only interested in clearing a place for a new idea.'

C: 'The question is capable of being answered "yes" or "no". In your literary criticisms, did you attack all the contemporary writers, be they called poets or versifiers?'

K: 'I did not attack them all. It is not true.'

On questioning by the judge, Costello explained that he

was attempting to show that 'every comment in the profile in *The Leader* was based on something written in this man's works'.

'Oh that is ridiculous,' Kavanagh responded, 'ridiculous. You might as well say that a man might be preaching a sermon in which he says, "if you sin, you will go to Hell". If you leave out the words "if you sin" you could say "didn't you say you will go to Hell".'

Costello replied: 'Maybe so. I will go through the article later on and I will show you that it refers to something in your articles.' He carried on, quoting from another of Kavanagh's pieces from *Envoy*: 'Everyone who is virtuous must believe in truth, and not be afraid to face it, and to accept with humility a derogatory judgment.' He asked Kavanagh: 'Would you accept with humility derogatory judgment of your works?'

'I am not worried about what anyone says about my works,' replied Kavanagh.

'You have brought a libel action because of what someone said about it,' Costello argued.

'I object most strongly to that,' counsel for Kavanagh intervened.

'It is an observation, Mr Costello,' Justice Teevan ruled.

K: 'I maintain that fair criticism is all right.'

C: 'Fair criticism, even if derogatory?'

K: 'If it is critical, I don't care how much it damages me. Any question of honest criticism, I will stand by.'

C: 'Do you expect fair criticism of your work even if it be derogatory?'

K: 'There is no use in saying these words. I am not a professor of phonetics.'

C: 'Do you accept fair criticism of your work even if such criticism be derogatory?'

K: 'I want to know exactly what you mean by derogatory?'

C: 'I am using your phrase, it is not my phrase.'

K: 'I don't like the word "derogatory" because we are both using it in different senses.'

Mr Kavanagh said that quite savage criticism had been made of him and he did not mind.

Justice Teevan clarified the point at issue: 'Mr Costello is asking you if you would object to that standard of criticism being applied to you, even if it meant speaking badly about you?'

'I don't mind, provided it is true. I don't mind what people say about me.'

'BIGGER FIELDS, HARDER ROCKS, DEEPER BOGS'

Costello moved on to a reference to the poet, Austin Clarke, in an article by Kavanagh. Was not Clarke 'a pretty good poet'?

'He was not included in *Twentieth-Century Verse* published by Faber,' answered Kavanagh.

'Is he considered by some to be a pretty good poet?' Justice Teevan asked.

'Some people consider the people who write on the back of *Old Moore's Almanac* to be pretty good poets,' Kavanagh replied.

'You were not asked that,' Justice Teevan pointed out. 'You were asked do some regard Mr Clarke as a pretty good poet?'

'I would like to know who "some" are,' replied Kavanagh.

'You are not as innocent as all that,' Costello accused. 'He is thought of sufficiently well by Radio Éireann for them to give him a post as commentator on literary matters.'

'I am not prepared to attack him here, and say anything derogatory about anybody,' said Kavanagh.

'You did it here in *Envoy*,' Costello pointed out and quoted from the article: 'His poetry talks on Dublin radio are interminable, a story without an end; poems of fields, poems of rocks, poems of bogs, poems of bigger fields, harder rocks, deeper bogs. Needless to say, I have never listened to these talks which, I believe, are usually illustrated by chanting verse speakers.'

The packed courtroom laughed in appreciation.

C: 'Isn't that pretty severe criticism of Mr Austin Clarke?'

K: 'It was not criticism of the man.'

C: 'You criticised the giving of a job to Mr Clarke in Radio Éireann.'

K: 'I suggested that they should transfer him to a job he was equipped for.'

C: 'You criticised the giving of a job?'

K: 'Because I believed in poetry as an important thing.'

C: 'You criticised him as not being fit for his job?'

K: 'No.'

Justice Teevan: 'Did you use that expression?'

K: 'I think in fairness …'

C: 'In the article that I have just quoted you use the words

I have been referring to. "This giving of the job to Clarke is yet another example of the patronage of mediocrity that we have had.'"

Justice Teevan: 'That is quite a different thing, Mr Costello.'

C: 'Weren't you suggesting, Mr Kavanagh, that Mr Austin Clarke was not a sufficiently good poet to be employed on the radio and to give talks on Radio Éireann about poetry in general, and Irish poetry in particular?'

K: 'I will answer it this way. What would doctors say about a quack that was given a job in Vincent's Hospital?'

C: 'That is the same standard?'

K: 'If he is not fit for the job he is not first class.'

C: 'And you regarded him as not being fit for the job.'

K: 'I would like him to get another job.'

'STRIPPED BARE WITH NO POSING'

C: 'What is your opinion of F.R. Higgins?'

K: 'He was not bad. He had merit, a little merit.'

C: 'In an article called "The Gallivanting Poet" you said that writing about Mr Higgins was "a problem – a problem of exploring a labyrinth that leads nowhere".'

K: 'I agree with that, yes.'

C: 'The writer of the profile article in *The Leader* used the word "labyrinth" about you?'

K: 'Yes.'

C: 'Those are pretty strong words.'

K: 'One literary man writing about another.'

C: 'Did you describe Mr Higgins' poetry as "sincere" when he was alive?'

K: 'I could hardly remember doing such a nonsensical thing.'

Costello quoted a longer excerpt from 'The Gallivanting Poet': 'Even the man's name is doubtful. Someone once told me that while travelling with Higgins in Meath the poet inquired of an old man regarding the great Irish family of Higginses and the old man said: "The name wasn't Higgins, it was Huggins and they were an English family." The whole point is that the name wouldn't have mattered a hoot – he could be called X, Y, Z – if he didn't himself think it mattered. And when he based his whole work on this heresy one can realise what a shadowy foundation and a shadowy building his achievement is.'

C: 'Is this not severe criticism?'

K: 'It is correct criticism.'

C: 'Were you not suggesting that he, Mr Higgins was really a Huggins and, therefore, an English Protestant?'

K: 'No, that is not correct. What I objected to was Higgins and all that school playing the romantic Irishmen when, in fact, at heart, if they were sincere, they were hard-headed people and there was nothing romantic about them. This was an act, posing as romantics. That is what I objected to.'

Costello resumed his quotations: 'Personally, Higgins was like his verse. He carried the gallivanting pose into ordinary life. He pronounced poetry as "poertry" and drawled humorously. One gets weary of such posing and longs for the simple reality of a man. I hate being cruel to his memory, but I cannot get away from the fact that he never became adult and sincere.'

Costello asked: 'Is this not criticism of Higgins himself, and not of his poetry or works?'

K: 'In fact, I think it is remarkably good criticism, if I may say so myself – very sincere and written with great passion.'

C: 'You said you never attacked people personally. Isn't this an attack, to say that Higgins was like his verse. You already said he was insincere in his verse.'

K: 'I think he was both. I have stated my point of view on this very well. You should be yourself, stripped bare with no posing.'

C: 'Do you agree that that is a criticism of his personality, as distinct from his poetry?'

K: 'I was writing historically. I wasn't writing for somebody alive. That is a different angle.'

C: 'Do you agree that that is a criticism of his personality, as distinct from his poetry?'

K: 'He lived that kind of way.'

Costello referred to Kavanagh's description of Robaird Ó Faracháin [Robert Farren]: 'He is an interesting example of how far a man can get through sheer industry, unsupported by sensibility. I often read his verses and wondered would he ever succeed through weight of words in striking the divine chord. It was a consolation to know that these sorts of accidents don't happen.'

He then asked: 'Was not this rather harsh?'

Kavanagh explained that it was commonplace literary criticism.

The court broke for lunch. Costello had spent the entire morning grinding away at Kavanagh, slowly wearing him down, implementing the defence approach. They were trying to portray him as a man who could dish out criticism but could not take it.

'The dead and damned to dullness'

After lunch the cross-examination resumed. An article in *Envoy* dated June 1951 next came under the scrutiny of Mr Costello. There was some discussion about what sort of article it was.

'Is it,' the judge asked, 'a résumé of your views on Irish poets?'

'I think I would never be guilty of a résumé,' Kavanagh replied.

That settled, Costello quoted from the article: '"One of the things it would be necessary to teach in this country is that the pygmy literature that was produced by the so-called Irish Literary Renaissance is quite worthless." Does that express your views as to the Irish Literary Revival from Yeats onwards?'

'No man ever expresses his entire complex view in a phrase. It is part of my point of view,' replied Kavanagh.

'What is regarded as literary? The Abbey Theatre, Yeats and the rest of them?'

'That is a queer mixture,' Kavanagh declared to much

laughter. 'I did not mention Yeats.'

C: 'That is what you'd call "pygmy literature".'

K: 'I did not say Yeats.'

C: 'Is he not part of the Irish Literary Renaissance?'

K: 'No, Yeats is Yeats. In the last analysis I would not include him.'

Kavanagh went on to state that Yeats had described such contemporary poets as a 'lot of fleas eating off his back'.

C: 'Who do you call the "fleas"?'

K: 'The mediocre.'

C: 'Who did Yeats consider mediocre?'

K: 'I could not say offhand.'

C: 'Did you not write, "what may be called the Abbey Theatre's school of writers had practically no merit beyond the background"?'

K: 'I agree. That is correct.'

Costello quoted a longer extract: 'Every organ of opinion in Ireland today is in the hands of the enemies of the imagination. The most pernicious enemies are those which have pretensions to culture, such as *The Irish Times*, which has a large weekly literary page in which the dead and damned to dullness express themselves. Poor Mr Smyllie, the editor, is not to blame entirely: it is generally believed that he has little power ... What is most appalling here is that the government controlled radio station, supported out of the taxes, is in the hands of mean little men who are partial to their own pathetic point of view ...'

He then focused on one point: 'You say that Radio Éireann is in the hands of mean little men.'

K: 'As a matter of fact, the policy was changed as a result of my activities.'

Laughter from the public.

'There must be silence in court,' Justice Teevan announced. 'It would be impossible to conduct the case otherwise.'

C: 'Do you know that a number of Irish people with pretensions to some poetic quality have had works from time to time accepted and published in the literary page of *The Irish Times*?'

K: 'I'll answer the first part of that question – I believe there is no one in Ireland without literary pretensions.'

C: 'I have not any.'

K: 'I have written in *The Irish Times* myself.'

C: 'These people who have their work accepted by *The Irish Times* think this is an indication that it is of some artistic merit?'

K: 'It might be.'

C: 'Would you not think that these people who work hard at artistic prose would be entitled to take offence at your comprehensive condemnation of them in your phrase, "the dead and the damned to dullness express themselves"?'

K: 'It is an opinion I am perfectly entitled to. It is real criticism.'

C: 'I am not objecting to your opinion. We have in the constitution that everybody is entitled to free expression of opinions. What I am referring to is your use of a very strong phrase. Do you not think these people would be entitled to take offence from this phrase?'

K: 'The implication in my statement is that there is a

world of goodness and of merit which has denied them its existence.'

Since Kavanagh had not answered the question Costello repeated it.

C: 'Are not people entitled to take offence?'

K: 'I am dealing with the world of aesthetics. There must be someone, some authority to deliver the final judgment.'

C: 'If you, as a literary critic, are entitled to indulge in that class of very strong criticism, surely you, as a poet yourself, subject to criticism, should be able to take it as well as these people?'

Kavanagh replied: 'I believe that only the man who has earned the right has the right to be wrong. Whereas if you have no right you must definitely be on the side of truth. I know that the only person in whom error is tolerated is a great genius, talking his head off.'

'I have not the remotest idea what you are talking about,' Costello confessed.

'I am talking about people who are very bad, being told they are the greatest in the world. Yeats praised outrageously, knowing that it did not matter,' answered Kavanagh.

Justice Teevan intervened, again asking about Kavanagh's attitude to criticism.

'I would not be one bit vexed about criticism that is fair and honest. Criticism deals with the world of ideas. It is all ideas. There are no persons there at all,' Kavanagh insisted. 'I was fair, I am fair and will be fair in the future.'

Finally Mr Costello got around to the central matter at hand. He read the first paragraph of the profile and asked Kavanagh what he objected to in it.

K: 'It is the perfect portrait of a pervert – some atrocious person. It is ridiculous.'

C: 'May we take it step-by-step? You don't see anything wrong with a description of you sitting on a stool in a bar?'

K: 'In that context, very much. If you isolate it from the context it is perfectly all right.'

C: 'Do you habitually go to public houses in Dublin?'

K: 'Occasionally.'

C: 'It is alleged that we have accused you in that paragraph of being of intemperate habits.'

K: 'It is in there. It is the whole build-up of that paragraph. It is a monstrous paragraph. It is a net of villainy … The whole paragraph is villainous. I read into it the implication that I am intemperate and everybody else who spoke to me about it said the same. The whole impression is that I am almost never out of pubs.'

C: 'There has hardly been an article you write in which you do not refer to pubs.'

K: 'Maybe so.'

Costello moved on to the allegation in the plaintiff's statement of case where it was said that the profile made him out to be a 'sponger'. He asked where in the article that was stated. Was he not shown in the article ordering a drink for himself?

'The innuendo is clear that I did not pay for it that I am the master who orders people around,' said Kavanagh. 'The implication was that I was a "sponger" in that I was a master of those slaves and did not buy them a drink.'

Costello went on to quote an article in *Envoy* in which

Kavanagh holds a conversation with himself: 'There is also the BBC, which is quite friendly to you, and there are scores of journals in America if you were not too damned lazy. Ah, Kavanagh, I'll never make a man of you. Stick to your typewriter. Don't mind that call to the door asking you out to the pub, to waste your time and his money.'

Kavanagh explained that these were two characters in an imaginative piece of work. As to what relation that passage had to himself, Kavanagh explained: 'It is imaginative writing. It has nothing to do with reality. You might as well take Agatha Christie who writes murder stories, and accuse her of the murder in one of her books.'

Costello persisted: 'Are there two people involved in the soliloquy?'

K: 'Two characters.'

C: 'Was one of them Patrick Kavanagh?'

K: 'No. He might be one but there are many.'

C: 'How many?'

K: 'Two characters.'

C: 'Were you both Kavanagh?'

K: 'There were two Kavanaghs.'

C: 'One was Kavanagh getting the advice.'

K: 'Yes, but who was giving it?'

Laughter in the court.

Costello next targeted the Palace and the Pearl, quoting Kavanagh again: 'As soon as one begins to consider the social landscape of literary Ireland today, one is liable to fall into the error of thinking about the Palace and the Pearl bars on Friday evening. These pubs are the haunts of newspapermen;

Mr R.M. Smyllie will not like the distinction: for I gather that the leaders in his paper are not written in journalese, but in prose. When I came to Dublin in 1939, I thought the Palace the most wonderful temple of art. That's where the gabble of poetry was to be heard.'

Mr Costello asked the witness to clarify if 'Mr R.M. Smyllie is the editor of *The Irish Times*?'

'He is, I believe,' Kavanagh replied and went on to explain: 'The only reason I went into these bars, the Palace and the Pearl was that you got a means of contact with anyone who could give me work. I would have preferred to sit in a café although I would like a pint of stout or a glass of whiskey as much as anyone.'

Costello asked, 'Do you remember seeing a cartoon by an Australian artist [Alan Reeve]?'[2]

Kavanagh replied, 'I saw it.'

'And you figure prominently and dominantly in that?'

'He put me at the back with a man who never was in a pub,' said Kavanagh, adding that in any case the cartoon was made in a studio up town. He explained his presence again: 'You would want to be in the swim.'

C: 'That is the only reason? You had to be there to get a job?'

K: 'On reflection, I would say that I also went into those bars for company.'

C: 'The company of artists?'

K: 'Any company at all is good enough for me. Good company does not necessarily have to be artists.'

C: 'You went there because there were plenty of artists?'

K: 'I wish there were not.'

C: 'It was the artistic, the so-called intelligentsia of Dublin.'

K: 'I discovered it was totally bogus.'

C: 'Bogus?'

K: 'Yes, quite ridiculous.'

'THE GABBLE OF POETRY'

Costello continued with his line of questioning: 'I am suggesting about this time that you were the dominant personality at those meetings in the Palace Bar of the so-called intelligentsia of Dublin.'

'Indeed I was not. I was an obscure personality,' Kavanagh said and added, 'anyone who doesn't think that was very foolish'.

Asked if he had not taken part in controversy in the Palace Bar at the time, Kavanagh replied that 'it was just a pub where nobody was important'.

'Does the phrase "that's where the gabble of poetry was to be heard" not suggest that there was a great deal of talk in the Palace about poetry?' pressed Costello.

Kavanagh replied: 'I cannot have heard that if I was such a dominant personality on that stage. Was I doing the gabbling?'

On being asked by Costello did he agree that the patronage of the intelligentsia had shifted from the Palace Bar to McDaid's of Harry Street, Kavanagh said he did not: 'I know McDaid's which was close to the office of the *Envoy*, and when the profile in *The Leader* referred to McQuaid's I knew the reference was to McDaid's … It was totally isolated. *Envoy* was totally isolated.'

C: 'Don't you agree that you, being one of the outstanding figures in Irish literary life, had a number of disciples?'

K: 'I don't like to use that word. I had people of all ages who knew I did stand for honesty and sincere thinking.'

C: 'Did you have a number of people who looked up to you as the great figure in Irish literary life?'

K: 'I would say about … fifty thousand.'

C: 'And that fifty thousand drifted in to look at the master in McDaid's Pub in Harry Street?'

K: 'They would be more likely to find me in Mitchell's Café than in McDaid's.'

C: 'Were there a number of poets or would-be poets trying to get you to write and praise their poetry?'

K: 'No. I hardly ever spoke about literature or poetry in public.'

C: 'What did you speak about in the presence of all the artists?'

K: 'Sport.'

In answer to further questions about literary company in pubs, Mr Kavanagh replied: 'When I came up from a small farm, I thought it was marvellous to get into such high society.'

C: 'But you found they were all sham?'

K: 'I found they were not the kind of thing that interested me after a few years.'

C: 'Why?'

K: 'Well, it is a long story. You cannot analyse that.'

C: 'Those that had no poetic merit?'

K: 'No. I do not agree with you.'

C: 'I have quoted from your own works.'

K: 'I do not leave any man's company because he had no poetic merit.'

'I'LL PRAISE AND PRAISE AND SEE WHAT IT COMES TO'

Unlike the character in the profile who said: 'Yous have no merit, no merit at all', Kavanagh claimed that he did not discourage young people and, indeed, would 'encourage any person with the slightest speck of merit'.

C: 'You have no use for trash.'

K: 'With a young person, I'll praise and praise and see what it comes to. I do not condemn the young.'

C: 'Did you ever tell anyone that they had no literary merit?'

K: 'Who could be a writer and a critic and not say it sometime.'

Justice Teevan clarified: 'Have you written several times of some people that they had no merit, no literary merit?'

K: 'You are bound to say it. Something must be of no use sometime. It is quite obvious.'

Justice Teevan: 'That is what I want to establish.'

K: 'I'll admit that. I am a critic.'

Mr Costello resumed his questioning of Kavanagh's destructive criticism of other Irish writers, saying that he had written: 'There could hardly be said to be a decent poet in Ireland … It is I who have led a movement to sweep out the bogus thing that sprang from Synge and the Abbey Theatre. There is a new thing growing up – a fresh and lovely thing too.'

Costello asked if 'at the moment there isn't a genuine poet in the country?'

Kavanagh replied: 'There will be good writers in the country, and it will be due to my work.'

'Let us hope there will be. At the moment there wasn't a genuine one?' asked Costello.

'I would say so.'

Costello quoted from a Kavanagh poem 'Bank Holiday': 'In the pubs for seven years men have given him their ears, buying the essence of his heart with a porter-perfumed fart.'

Costello asked Kavanagh to explain: 'Doesn't that mean that for the price of a pint, a man was picking your poetic brain, "buying the essence of his heart"?'

Kavanagh explained that it was not that straightforward and went on to claim: 'The Devil can quote scripture and the Devil is doing it in this case.'

C: 'You being the scripture and I am the Devil?'

K: 'I do not want to be pushed too much. I meant you can, if evil-minded, you can draw evil. You can draw an evil conclusion from any data. If you are evil-minded you can take a little bit and frame it into something totally untrue.'

Mr Justice Teevan intervened: 'Mr Costello feels you are referring to him.'

K: 'Indeed I am not. I think he is a very saintly person.'

Evidently tiring of this line of inquiry Justice Teevan asked Costello if he was passing on to something else in his cross-examination.

'I am passing out,' Costello confessed.

'Are you finished with the witness?' asked Justice Teevan.

'Oh, not at all,' said Costello, 'I am passing out myself with fatigue.'

'Then we will adjourn until 11 o'clock tomorrow.'

Chapter 13

'I don't believe in facetiousness'

According to the *Evening Herald*, who headlined their front-page 'Women Throng Court to hear Libel Action':

> … fashionably dressed women and girls comprised a large portion
> of the crowd in the public gallery and waiting outside the High
> Court to hear the libel action today … Fifteen minutes before Mr
> Justice Teevan took his seat on the bench every seat in the public
> gallery was occupied and a queue extended around the central hall,
> waiting for admission to whatever space was available in the body
> of the court. Extra guards and officials were again present to ensure
> that those having business in the court could enter or leave.[1]

The Irish Times was similarly taken by the number of female
spectators, to judge by 'An Irishman's Diary':

> 'It is a good job,' said the Dublin theatrical manager fervently, 'that
> the courts don't sit in the evening. If they did, we might as well
> close down'. He spoke with feeling, having just previously cast an
> envious eye over the queues for the Kavanagh libel action. 'I know
> they don't have to pay,' he said, 'but there hasn't been a queue like
> it in Dublin since Maurice Chevalier played the Royal.'

EVENING HERALD

(INCORPORATING THE "EVENING TELEGRAPH")

Vol. 63. No. 34   DUBLIN, TUESDAY, FEBRUARY 9, 1954   Price Twopence

4/- LUNCH   4 COURSES
ROAST PORK
RUMP STEAK
BACON and CABBAGE
ROAST MUTTON
... and 3/6 Lunch
GREEN ROOSTER
(O'CONNELL ST.)

ptimism

y had been closed,
an sources said, because
ight had bothered the
ll's eyes.
morning the Pontiff
Mass, said at his private
t, and received Holy
ion. But he was not
le to resume saying Mass
lf.

OF
FOR

Wedding at
Howth To-day

**WOMEN THRONG
COURT TO HEAR
LIBEL ACTION**

FASHIONABLY dressed women and
girls comprised a large portion of the   ★

The Evening Herald *was intrigued by the number of women who
turned up to witness proceedings.*

More conservative habitués of the courts were reluctant to
admit that the previous day's queues were record-breakers,
but they did concede that only the most sensational Green
Street cases, as a rule, mustered a larger public, and few of
them recalled greater numbers of the public besieging the
scanty public accommodation afforded in a High Court case.
'An Irishman's Diary' went on to say:

Indeed the normal austerity of the High Court had yesterday
some of the quality of the transformation scene in a pantomime.
Perhaps the deceptive weather (yesterday had the balminess of a
spring day) had something to do with the unusual concentration
of fair women, who brought an element of the fashion parade to
the chamber of justice. Perhaps it was merely feminine curiosity
that brought so many of them. But if it were, they didn't neglect
their decorative instincts.

As for the brave men – the eve of Waterloo had nothing
on yesterday's assembly. Among the public, there were at least

3 TDs, 2 senators, a whole shoal of scholars and savants, poets,
professors, actors and actresses, and representatives of all the
learned and scientific professions, while outside the court the
queues waited hopefully, from mid-morn till dewy eve, anxious
to get in for even five minutes of the hearing.

The working part of the court – the stage area, as it were, was
less glamorous. Counsels' table looked for all the world like a
Saturday book-barrow on the quays. There seemed to be volumes
of every periodical and publication that has been published in or
about Ireland for the past ten years piled up including one copy
of an old *Irish Times*. The principal players too were sombre, in
contrast to their female audience.[2]

Even as the case continued, Costello was being congratulated
on his performance. John J. Hearne, Irish ambassador to the
United States, wrote in a private letter from Washington:
'you were at the top of your form in your cross-examination
of the plaintiff. We can't wait till today's papers arrive and
tomorrow's.'

Being a member of the Irish diplomatic service, which
had been famously attacked in *Kavanagh's Weekly*, Hearne
did not have a huge amount of sympathy for the poet: 'I am
sure it would be wrong for me to comment on the case itself.
My comments might create a new misdemeanour … even if
I were merely to say "Bah-ha" to or of and concerning the
plaintiff …'[3]

When the case opened, Mr T.J. Connolly for the plaintiff
rose and said that he proposed calling Doctor Thomas
Bodkin and asked permission for Mr Kavanagh's evidence
to be interrupted so that Professor Bodkin, the distinguished

authority on the arts could be called as a witness. Bodkin had been in Dublin since the previous Thursday and it was imperative for him to return to London.

'We could perhaps take him at two o'clock,' suggested Connolly. 'I mention it now to give timely notice.'

'That is the first I have heard of it,' Costello declared.

'Do you object?' the judge asked.

Costello replied: 'I will. I don't know what evidence Dr Bodkin proposes to give. There will be legal objection to the particular type of evidence.'

'Apart from that will it interfere with your defence?'

'I don't think anything Dr Bodkin says can interfere with my defence,' replied Costello.

'We'll say two o'clock, subject to any objections,' Justice Teevan finished.

Costello stated that, in any case, he did not want his cross-examination interrupted. Connolly, for the plaintiff, pointed out that it would be interrupted by the luncheon interval anyway.

'You may renew your application [to have the witness heard] at one o'clock,' Teevan decided.

Due to complaints of overcrowding and general discomfort fewer people were admitted to the court than in previous days and many who formed a queue throughout the morning failed to get in. Resuming his interrogation, Costello continued his strategy of taking Kavanagh through the phrases used in the profile and teasing out Kavanagh's objections to them. He asked about the choice of words, 'yous have no merit, no merit at all', which had appeared in *The Leader* article. Was this not an expression which he had habitually employed in his writings?

K: 'No, my Lord.'

C: 'Well, I find in this famous Diary of yours [in *Envoy*] that you use the word "yous" on at least two occasions.'

K: 'In an element of drollery.'

C: 'And isn't this an element of drollery?'

K: 'It is an element of vicious malice.'

C: 'In the August 1950 issue of *Envoy* had you written "did yous win itself?" about an imaginary football match. Do you remember that?'

K: 'Yes.'

C: 'I want to show you were familiar with the expression.'

K: 'Yes, but I don't use it in literary criticism. That is a fair description of rural life and a football match.'

C: 'And people here in Dublin would say it is a facetious mood?'

K: 'The mood is what matters.'

C: 'In a facetious mood, you do it yourself?'

K: 'I don't use facetiousness. It is a very cheap form of humour. I don't believe in facetiousness.'

C: 'That is a pity.'

K: 'It is the humour of fools.'

C: 'The humour of fools …'

K: 'The humour of shallow people anyway. It is a sign of shallowness.'

C: 'Why do you use shallow?'

K: 'I don't use facetiousness.'

C: 'As to the Left Bank, referred to in *The Leader*, that is the poetic part of Paris, the left bank of the Seine, where poets, painters and artists congregate.'

K: 'I have heard it.'

C: 'Where artists, painters, poets and writers congregate in the cafés and talk art, literature, painting and poetry.'

K: 'I was never there.'

C: 'You never heard that much?'

K: 'I may have.'

C: 'And you have read books about it?'

K: 'I cannot say I did.'

C: 'As to the "sylph-like redheads and dewy-eyed brunettes", is there something wrong with the phrase?'

K: 'Yes, considerably wrong.'

When asked if he had been the editor of *Kavanagh's Weekly*, the witness replied, 'partly. Not fully editor.' He was then shown the first issue of the paper, containing the words 'edited by Patrick Kavanagh'.

K: 'Yes, edited by a person who was part-time because my brother who owned it and paid for it said that I would draw a larger audience and get greater readership than he would. But he was virtually editor.'

C: 'Did you have it registered as a newspaper?'

K: 'I could not say because I did not do it.'

C: 'But at all events, it says you are the editor?'

K: 'I do not know what he put down.'

C: 'Were you deceiving the public?'

K: 'Not to that extent. I had a good deal to do with it anyway.'

C: 'And did you write under the "Graftonia" column in *Kavanagh's Weekly*?'

K: 'Bits of it.'

Asked if he had not written, in the seventh issue of the *Weekly* Kavanagh replied: 'A charge has been made against me.'

He continued: 'I cannot remember. It is the editorial "we".'

C: 'No, it is "me".'

K: 'It is "me" in that case, but this was a column written by various hands and we used "me" or "we" to give the impression that it was a one-man job.'

C: 'Is the "charge against me" referred to against you?'

K: 'It is against Graftonia, a mythical person who wrote that column. My brother paid me a salary and as such, the man who paid the piper called the tune in regard to responsibility.'

C: 'I don't think that is the usual policy of newspapers. Isn't the editor given a free hand in matters of general policy?'

K: 'I have already stated in another article that editors do not have that power.' Kavanagh, in response to further questioning agreed that in the *Weekly* he had used a poem of Byron's dealing with sylph-like brunettes: 'It is a beautiful and romantic verse,' he added, 'there are no flashy pubs about that.'

Costello proceeded to read from an article in *Kavanagh's Weekly*: '… when I think it is the warmest enthusiasm of women which gives me hope for the future of this country. To become wise a man should be a lot in the company of women: that is why I like being in cafés where women congregate. I also discovered that the better-looking women are, the wiser they are. There is probably a reason for this; women are magnets which draw wisdom, and they draw their wisdom through men, so it follows that the more attractive a woman is the more she is likely to draw wisdom; for in the first place she can afford to be selective and have as male friends only fairly intelligent ones.'

When it seemed as if Costello was going to leave it at that, Kavanagh asked the judge if he was entitled to comment on the difference between this passage and the reference in the profile to 'sylph-like redheads and dewy-eyed brunettes.'

'The kind of women …' Kavanagh said.

'I would prefer you would not do that,' the judge warned. 'Comment on the two texts, that of the profile and the excerpt read out just now by Mr Costello. It is only fair to comment on the difference between them.'

Kavanagh responded: 'The fact of the matter is, I am not interested in, and I dislike very much, the kind of people referred to in the profile. I would like to know only decent people, ordinary, intelligent, simple people. This is the people I am referring to in the Graftonia article. Good women.'

'Are you suggesting to the jury,' Costello asked, 'that ladies who are not interested in poetry and arts do not go into what you call these poets' pubs here in Dublin.'

K: 'I do not like the hangers-on of art.'

C: 'Perhaps you don't like what you call the hangers-on of art, but do ladies who are interested in poetry and art and literature go in there?'

K: 'They certainly would not be expected to by me.'

C: 'But they go in? Answer the question!'

K: 'I would not answer that they go in. I'd say they do not go in. The women I am interested in. According to my definition they do not go in.'

C: 'I want to know, do ordinary, decent women who are interested in art and poetry and literature go in where poets and artists and other people frequent a certain public house in the city of Dublin?'

K: 'I would say it is very doubtful, in my opinion, if they do.'

C: 'I asked you for a fact. I'll test your memory on this.'

K: 'I'll say the truth. I do not like women who go into pubs and hang around over art. I always feel the art is the subsidiary thing.'

C: 'Whether it is or not, will you now answer the question? Do ladies interested in art and poetry go into the pubs where you were – McDaid's, the Palace Bar and other places? Do they go in, whether you like it or not?'

K: 'I can explain it quite simply. I have been asked do ladies interested in art, literature and poetry go into pubs. I deny those ladies I saw were interested in these things. They were interested in something else and using it as an excuse.'

C: 'Will you answer the question I put to you?'

K: 'I say no.'

Further pressed, Kavanagh explained: 'It is only an excuse. They are not interested in art and letters. Women that I knew interested in these subjects never went there.'

C: 'Isn't it a fact that respectable women go into public houses in Dublin and elsewhere?'

K: 'I quite agree with you.'

Costello, at long last decided that he had got enough mileage out of the 'sylph-like redheads in pubs' and turned instead to the profile and Shelley's 'pard-like spirit, beautiful and swift'. He asked Kavanagh if this was applicable to him.

K: 'No, it was gratuitous, unmannerly and leering.'

C: 'Have you any objection to your mind being described as "a labyrinthine jungle"?'

K: 'I certainly have. You yourself admitted yesterday that my mind was not labyrinthine.'

C: 'Yet you have no objection to using the phrase "labyrinthine" about the late Mr Higgins?'

K: 'It is perfectly true.'

Justice Teevan asked if the phrase 'labyrinthine jungle' had been used by Mr Kavanagh about Mr Higgins.

'It certainly was not,' Mr Connolly for the plaintiff replied.

Next up for consideration was a reference by Kavanagh to Seán O'Faolain. He had used the phrase 'the weedy growth of his mind' about Mr O'Faolain.

K: 'I was writing about Mr O'Faolain's work.'

C: 'The profile article was dealing with your work.'

K: 'I don't agree.'

C: 'Isn't it dealing as much with your work as when you said, "writing about Mr Higgins is a problem – a problem of exploring a labyrinth that leads nowhere"?'

K: 'I was writing historically about a man who had died.'

C: 'When you wrote about the late Mr F.R. Higgins, "as accepting the fraudulent premises and invalid symbols established by the subject", you were writing about a dead man who could not have answered back?'

K: 'I could not take the dinner off his table either. It did no damage.'

C: 'And when you referred to "the maze of weedy detail which is O'Faolain's mind"…?'

K: 'I think it is my duty to say that. That is said in serious criticism.'

C: 'If you are entitled to say that, surely the author of this profile is entitled to use the same approach in getting at your mentality?'

K: 'It is not dealing with my works.'

For his next exercise, Costello turned to an article about the plaintiff by Hubert Butler in *The Bell*, in which it was stated: 'Mr Kavanagh's mind, when he abandons poetry, is like a monkey house at feeding time.'

'Yes, read it all,' the witness protested, 'it is quite a critical article, written at a high level and it is true criticism by a serious man. I liked it very much. It is an excellent article. Read it all. It is written on a high level of seriousness.'

Turning to what Kavanagh had written about truth, Costello said: 'The world is full of Pilates, asking the question which is always cynical "what is truth?" and any man who has in him something of Christ will reply, "I am truth" before he is led off to starvation.'

'I don't see anything wrong with that,' Kavanagh said. 'I hope we all have something of Christ in us, Mr Costello.'

'I believe we have,' counsel for the defence agreed. He then went on to ask, 'is it not a legitimate comment on the passage quoted that you regard yourself as the ultimate truth.'

K: 'I do not.'

C: 'But another person might take the view from that phrase?'

K: 'Of course, that is pure Christianity, but it is also pure Thomism.'

C: 'What is that?'

K: 'It comes from St Thomas Aquinas. The point about that is that it is pure Christianity.'

C: 'I am not saying it isn't.'

K: 'I want to explain that to you.'

'Keep it as short as you can,' Mr Justice Teevan implored.

Kavanagh began: 'St Thomas Aquinas speaks not of reason, but of the Divine Intelligence – the flash – and that is the flash I am talking about – the truth. He says you don't arrive at it through pure reasoning. I am talking of Divine Intelligence, different from reason.'

'Do you agree that literary criticism allows people to express their views, good bad and indifferent on a writer and this is enshrined in the Constitution?' asked Costello.

'No man has a right to intrude into another man's private soul,' replied Kavanagh.

'I am going to try to help you, certainly to help the jury,' Costello said to Kavanagh.

When Mr Costello stated that he was going to try to help the witness, Mr Connolly interjected loudly: 'Beware!'

As regards the attitude of the witness to Dublin, Costello quoted from the well-thumbed profile: 'Certainly until recently, he has always regarded the city with suspicion'.

K: 'That is nonsense.'

C: 'It may be nonsense, but a person is entitled to write nonsense, and it is not defamatory.'

K: 'It suggests that I dislike Dublin and it is not true. I love the place. I have always done so. Why should I come and stay in it if I didn't?'

C: 'That passage may be untrue, but the writer is entitled to take an untrue view of your works.'

K: 'He is not talking about my works. He is talking about a cunning rascal coming down the street suspicious of everybody.'

Costello then referred to a passage from *The Green Fool*. Kavanagh said there was some fact and fiction in that book, he had said so before. That book was written under the old romantic school: 'You cannot go back to a man's childhood. I changed after that. I do not like that book.'

'How does anybody know that?' Costello asked.

'I said it in writing. You would not get a copy of that book now, even in the National Library. I don't stand over *The Green Fool*,' replied Kavanagh. 'I could use a famous quotation. It was not that I loved Dublin less but that I loved my rural place more,' Kavanagh explained.

'That is what the writer of the article in *The Leader* is suggesting,' answered Costello.

'No,' Kavanagh replied, 'love is a thing that has no clouds in it.'

Costello read an extract from *Envoy* [Tale of Two Cities]:

And once again he gripped my hand in his
And said there was no place like Dublin.
His friendship wounded, but I dare not complain
For that would seem boorish. Yet it was this
Insincere good-nature that hurt me in Dublin
... Once again he would return to Dublin
Where among the failures he would pass unnoticed,

Happy in pubs talking about yesterday's wits,
And George Moore's use of the semi-colon …

Costello asked: 'Is it a poem?'

Kavanagh replied: 'I think it is – a very good one.'

Costello suggested that it showed the witness, viewing with critical eyes a Dublin exile he had met in a Fleet Street bar in London because the man was too fond of Dublin. 'Is that a possible interpretation?'

'No, there is the element of satire,' said Kavanagh and added: 'Don't worry; I like Dublin just the same. A man has no right to write what he purports to be a profile that has not read and taken a comprehensive view of my various writings.'

'Doesn't the constitution give him the right to free speech providing it does not contradict morality?' Costello asked. Justice Teevan intervened and Costello explained what he was doing.

'What I am getting at,' said Costello, 'is that you have mentioned Dublin in derogatory phrases in certain parts of your works and the writer of the profile article in *The Leader* was entitled to say that you do not seem to like Dublin, that you do not seem to like cities.'

'I disliked the Dublin that up to some time recently existed, a Dublin in which there was a considerable amount of malice, the kind of thing contained in that profile. That is the Dublin. It isn't my Dublin,' replied Kavanagh.

Asked what he meant by the phrase in one of his articles, 'the defeated don't rule in London as they do in Dublin', Kavanagh replied: 'It is purely philosophical. It must be read as an incantation. There is a question mark after every line although it isn't there. The kind of person who would read that would know.'

C: 'What do you mean by "the defeated"?'

K: 'It is very hard to say. It is very hard to analyse exactly.'

C: 'You can read it any way you like, but will you tell His Lordship and the jury what you mean.'

K: 'You might as well try to define the phrase, "a rose-red city half as old as time".'

C: 'Surely we all know what that means.'

K: 'You do not. I do not.'

Kavanagh explained that he had meant his reference to Dublin as a satire on the city, showing that he wanted to improve it: 'It is meant as a lover of Dublin who wanted it to be better … Satire is born of love, as you would know if you read Swift, who wrote the Drapier Letters and who was the greatest lover of Dublin.'

'He left the little wealth he had to found a home for the mad and showed by one satiric touch, no nation needed it so much,' Costello quoted. He then added: 'We are all mad?'

'That is from a lover of Dublin and a great man,' said Kavanagh.

Costello wisely left this alone and moved on to another of Kavanagh's poems: '"Could I go over the fields to the City of Kings/where art, music, letters are the real things/the stones of the street, the hedges high. No/earth, earth …" In the last part the stones cried out that you should go back to the country?'

'That is totally wrong,' replied Kavanagh. 'I am speaking mystically of God, of the City without Walls. It does not mean any mortal city. It means an immortal city. We are all earth born. We are trying to get into this place where wonderful imaginative things are, but the earth pulls us down. You would not put it in capital letters if it was not an immortal city.'

Justice Teevan added that he thought it was obvious that the reference was mystical. Costello replied he did not know what 'mystical' meant.

'I had better withdraw from this,' Justice Teevan said.

'I think we had all better withdraw,' Costello added.

Kavanagh referred to the city he mentioned in his poems as the 'eternal city' and Costello asked if he meant Rome.

Kavanagh replied: 'I did not mean Rome that is the eternal city. I meant the "immortal city".'

C: 'According to you, there is nothing very mystical about the eternal city – Rome.'

K: 'I thought you didn't know what mystical meant.'

'Rome, the actual city,' Mr Justice Teevan clarified.

K: 'Yes.'

C: 'In an article you wrote on Rome, you stated that in Rome there was "no intellectual light, all spectacle, distraction, no reflection. We can dismiss its millions without much comment for as a friend has remarked, Bogmen are the same everywhere".'

K: 'That was my reaction at the time.'

C: 'Anyone commenting on that would be entitled to say that you regarded cities with suspicion.'

K: 'I cannot be expected to answer for it now, it was written on my immediate reactions. Next day I might change my mind.'

As Costello attempted to quote further from the article on Rome, Kavanagh interrupted: 'You skipped a bit'.

Unabashed, Costello suggested that Kavanagh had sneered at Irish tourists to Rome in the article when he had referred to 'bogmen'.

'No one would call it that,' Kavanagh defended himself. 'You must get beneath the skin.' He said he was not sneering at his companions on their pilgrimage from Dublin to Rome: 'That is really an attempt at satire on the delusion that you can change yourself by changing your country or place.'

'What about, " ... we encountered gurriers speaking out of the corners of their mouth who wished to know if we wanted to change our money?" Do you object to the word taken from your own writing by the writer of the profile in *The Leader*?' Costello asked.

K: 'Those people in Rome were dealing in the black market in money.'

C: 'But you take exception to the use of the word in *The Leader* article?'

K: 'I certainly do. You could call me other things mentioned in my own writings and it would be very offensive. In my article on Rome I am dealing with black marketeers.'

Costello then went on to another piece in *Envoy*, 'Adventure in the Bohemian Jungle', in which the phrase 'Crumlin gurriers' had been used: '"At this point the satire explodes in a burst of wild cheering as the countryman joins a group of Crumlin gurriers who are betting on a competition for who can urinate the highest." So when you were dealing with "Crumlin gurriers", you were dealing with black marketeers?'

K: 'There are a lot of decent people in Crumlin.'

'I think they are all decent people in Crumlin,' the once and future Taoiseach replied.

'I protest against the reading of only a section of a work that is a complete work and has a complete impact. It is a long verse play and has a central impact,' protested Kavanagh.

'I cannot read it all as it is too long,' replied Costello.

Justice Teevan said that Mr Kavanagh was entitled to protest.

Costello argued that he was not, but that he could read the whole of the poem if he wished. He proceeded to read another extract: '"Count O'Mulligan brings with him two gross of gold, diamond-studded replicas of the Ardagh Chalice as cups to be competed for at the Drama Festival." Why bring the Ardagh Chalice into the description of a drunken scene?'

K: 'I have to bring it in to be true to myself. It was all part of the composite scene.'

Costello quoted: 'The Catholic Cultural League in procession headed by its chaplain, Father John, who is loaded down with two gross of rosary beads for presentation to the performers, moves slowly through.'

C: What was the point of bringing the Ardagh Chalice and the Catholic Cultural League into a scene like that?'

K: 'It was essential.'

C: 'Is there anything in that which leads to the conclusion you come to at the end about the Crumlin gurrier?'

'Every bit of it leads to it from the beginning to the end,' said Kavanagh and quoted some lines from the piece himself:

'This is the entrance to the bohemian jungle which lies on the perimeter of commerce.'

C: 'From the depths of the rotten vegetation can be heard the screams of drunken girls.'

K: 'The central thing is that attack on Dublin Bohemian life and the red-headed sylphs.'

C: 'Why bring Fr John and the rosary beads into a thing like that?'

K: 'Ah well, he had to come in for contrast.'

Laughter in the court.

K: 'I tried to portray life as it is and improve it.'

Costello asked about Kavanagh's comparison of Rome with London in his article: 'London, with its intellectual life, its inquiring mind, its adventurous publishers and its aristocratic belief in the importance of the poet.'

Kavanagh agreed that he had written this.

C: 'Will you agree that in the quotations I have given from your works about Dublin you regarded Dublin as being inferior from the intellectual point of view to London?'

K: 'No, I never regarded one collection of houses as being inferior to another collection.'

C: 'Do you regard London as superior to Dublin just as you regard London as being superior to Rome from an intellectual point of view?'

K: 'Of course, London is a big place. It is the head of the English-speaking world. If I am a writer, London would be most important. All the publishers are there. I regard London as bigger because there are more people in it.'

Justice Teevan asked what the relevance of this line of

questioning was and Mr Costello stated that Sir John Esmonde, for the plaintiff, had thrown down this article to the jury and said it was defamatory and that he must go through every line of it to prove it was not defamatory. Justice Teevan said he could understand the relevance of comparisons between rural and city life but not comparisons between cities.

By way of an explanation Costello asked Kavanagh if 'anyone reading your works would be entitled to comment that at one time you did not like cities and then you came to like them?'

'None could say that. I pulled up my roots which caused me pain, and came to the city,' replied Kavanagh. He added that he preferred London as a writer only and Dublin to live in.

Costello questioned Kavanagh about a paragraph in *The Leader* profile in which the writer depicted the poet in an imaginary room with a number of famous English poets.

Kavanagh agreed that John Betjeman was 'a very good poet' and that W.H. Auden was 'one of the greatest of living poets'. In the profile Kavanagh was described as 'day-dreaming himself into a world where there was aristocratic belief in the importance of the poet'. Costello then read an extract from a piece of Kavanagh's in *Envoy* 'that describes you as day-dreaming about all the hopes you had for the future?'

To which Kavanagh replied: 'Not at all, that is an entirely illiterate attitude to pick up.'

'I have been accused of many things, but this is the first time I have been accused of being illiterate,' defended Costello.

Laughter in the courtroom.

Kavanagh rested his head in his hands. His counsel, Mr Connolly asked if he was all right and Kavanagh was given a drink of water. The cross-examination continued. Costello asked again about London with 'its adventurous publishers and its aristocratic belief in the importance of the poet'. He pointed out that this depicted Kavanagh day-dreaming himself into an intellectual life in London.

'Why would I bother day-dreaming?' said Kavanagh. 'They are all friends of mine practically.'

Time for lunch. Connolly again reminded the judge of his request to allow Professor Bodkin give testimony. The judge said he would consider it.

'HE IS NO FRIEND OF MINE AND NEVER WAS'

When the court resumed after lunch Mr Connolly again raised the matter of Professor Thomas Bodkin. Connolly wished to make an application for Bodkin to give evidence for the plaintiff in the afternoon session. Mr Costello stated that Mr William O'Brien Fitzgerald, then cross-examining in another court, was interested in hearing this argument and would not be available for another twenty minutes. Justice Teevan said he would give the matter due consideration and deferred it for an hour.

After the break Costello resumed his quotations from Kavanagh's writings. He explained to the court why he was doing it: because it was necessary to show that the profile was an article of serious character, based as it was on a close reading of Mr Kavanagh's works.

C: 'This morning, I was at the point that, from an intellectual point of view, you prefer London to Dublin.'

K: 'I do not prefer London to Dublin.'

C: 'From an intellectual point of view?'

K: 'That is not true; I prefer to live in Dublin. It is a necessity to go to London every so often.'

C: 'Is there a better chance for an author of your calibre in London than in Dublin?'

K: 'There are publishers there, and a lot of big newspapers.'

Costello cited a passage from *Envoy*: 'Actually from an intellectual viewpoint the north has much greater freedom. For one thing it has the benefit of the BBC. The key to intellectual freedom is to leave it alone … Our best hope of salvation is England and the six counties.'

K: 'I was pro-partition then, but I am not now.'

C: 'Put that out of your head straight away. It has nothing to do with it at all.'

K: 'I am from the border. I originated there.'

C: 'Forget the border. It has nothing to do with it.'

Costello was keen to move away from any discussion of party politics. He turned to a quote from an article by Kavanagh in *Envoy* in which reference was made to a party in the Irish Club in London: 'To give some idea of the horror of it all, a man, dashing up the stairs, teetotaller too, wearing a pin, shouts at me, "How's Shakespeare?" The horror of it all.'

'What is wrong with that? Would you feel like giving a man like that a dig in writing, who had said such a vulgar thing as that? It was a barbarous statement.'

'Have you no sense of humour?' queried Costello.

'There's not much chance of using it here,' Kavanagh retorted, to much laughter in the court.

'Do you think this man with the teetotal pin was doing anything but making a bit of a joke as he was passing by?' asked Costello.

'He was being rude.'

Costello moved on to the subject of the plaintiff's relationship with Brendan Behan. The questioning grew heated.

C: 'Brendan Behan is mentioned in the profile. He was a friend of yours?'

K: 'He never was.'

C: 'Did he not distemper [paint] your flat?'

K: 'A man came in and did the plumbing also.'

C: 'Did he distemper your flat?'

K: 'I knew him as a painter. He is no friend of mine and never was.'

C: 'I suggest he was for some time.'

K: 'Never was a friend of mine.'

C: 'Why are you so hot about it?'

Kavanagh did not answer.

C: 'Do you disagree?'

K: 'I have said here and now that that man was never a friend of mine. He was never a friend of mine and he has never been a friend of mine. He is no friend of mine and never was a friend of mine. Have I to state it again? Never was a friend of mine.'

C: 'Did he distemper your flat?'

K: 'A painter distempered my flat.'

C: 'Was his name Brendan Behan?'

K: 'So they say. I had a painter in painting my flat.'

C: 'I suggest to you the Brendan Behan who came in to paint your flat was a friend of yours, and did it for nothing.'

K: 'He is no friend of mine. He is a friend of your friends that you are appearing for. I do not want him as a friend. I can choose my friends. My Lord, I don't want to be dragged into saying anything about any other man's character here in this court, but it is enough for me to say that I can choose my friends. That is all I say. That man never was, and never would be, a friend of mine. Is that a sufficient answer?'

Justice Teevan stated: 'That should be accepted.'

Costello disagreed: 'It is for the jury to accept. I am pressing you on it, Mr Kavanagh. I am not suggesting that you cannot choose your friends. I am suggesting, and have got an admission from you, that it was Brendan Behan who distempered your flat?'

'And I can tell you the name of the man who did my plumbing,' Kavanagh shot back. 'His name was Jack Smith, and I know another man who repaired the doors. His name was John Doyle.'

C: 'Are you suggesting that you paid Brendan Behan for distempering the flat just as an outside tradesman?'

K: 'Exactly.'

C: 'I put it to you that he was a friend of yours and distempered your flat.'

K: 'No.'

C: 'At all events, he distempered your flat.'

K: 'In some way, when I didn't know anything about him, I

allowed him to come in and distemper the flat. I did not want him. I like to keep the place a bit clean.'

C: 'I want to suggest he was a friend of yours and he fell out with you.'

K: 'That is a lie. It is a disgraceful lie.'

'He is getting more emphatic every time, Mr Costello,' Justice Teevan pointed out.

'It is a rotten lie that such a person is a friend of mine,' Kavanagh declared. 'I have chosen my friends from the noble and virtuous.'

C: 'Have you?'

K: 'Yes I have.'

C: 'That is interesting.'

K: 'That is part of the libel of the article.'

Next, Costello cited a cartoon from *Envoy* and some more quotations in his endeavour to show that phrases in the profile in *The Leader* were taken from Kavanagh's writings. Kavanagh took exception to the reading of one of them: 'Dead loves that were born for me.'

'Not well said,' Kavanagh commented, 'very badly spoken.'

'I am not a poet. I am only a working barrister,' replied Costello.

Once the defence moved on to *Kavanagh's Weekly* a legal argument ensued as to what was 'fair comment' and what was fact. The jury retired. Mr Justice Teevan took the opportunity to say that he was prepared to allow Professor Bodkin to give evidence.

'I object very strongly that a witness should be inserted into the tail-end of my cross-examination,' Costello argued.

Defence's point was that Bodkin's evidence, if admissible might change the course of the cross-examination that was in progress.

'It might upset the whole course of the trial,' Mr Fitzgerald newly returned from another courtroom stated. Justice Teevan said, that in view of such strong protest, he would not allow Bodkin to give evidence.

The professor, who had been sitting in the body of the court, left shortly afterwards. Professor Bodkin had been director of the National Gallery in Ireland before being appointed director of the newly-established Barber Institute of Fine Arts in Birmingham. John Ryan was also due to be called as a character witness. Ryan was no fan of Bodkins. As he put it himself: 'There was a mutual loathing between us, though we sat side-by-side for nearly two weeks. As it turned out, we were never called to give evidence.'[4]

Connolly took the chance of the break in proceedings to ask the judge to issue a subpoena for the production of the Register of Prohibited Publications for 1942, in order to show that the issue of *Horizon* that had contained 'The Great Hunger' had not been banned in Ireland. Justice Teevan granted the application and the jury was recalled.

Costello resumed his dissection of the profile article and its references to *Kavanagh's Weekly*. He read: 'few things, indeed, were favoured in it while it lasted and it was obvious that the Irish nation was regarded with a particular amount of disfavour ...'

K: 'Yes.'

C: 'Do you agree?'

K: 'Why would I? It is totally untrue. It was a most enthusiastic and generous paper, full of depth and passion and full of real belief in Ireland.'

C: 'Do you agree you criticised institutions and a number of leading people in the country?'

K: 'Undoubtedly there was criticism in it.'

C: 'Very strong.'

K: 'I cannot say very strong.'

Costello said that it was alleged that the profile had called Kavanagh shallow.

K: 'How would you like to be called shallow?'

C: 'Who would? I would not like to be accused of shallowness, unless I was shallow.'

K: 'I suppose you would like to accuse me of being shallow.'

C: 'I am here as counsel and am not accusing you of anything. I suggest that *you* have no hesitation in calling people shallow.'

Costello went on to quote from the very first issue of *Kavanagh's Weekly* dated 12 April 1952: 'While apologising for our necessary generalising at this juncture we may draw attention to some other not-always recognised facts. One is that the majority of politicians everywhere are fools or at any rate shallow people. In the fierce light that beats about the throne of those in power we are apt to forget that the politician giving out his weight about finance and other lofty affairs is quite ignorant of the subjects.'

'So,' concluded Costello, 'you had no hesitation in stating that all politicians were fools or, at any rate, shallow people.'

'I do not remember. It depends on the whole context.'

Costello continued to quote: 'Take for instance, Mr Lemass who is being groomed to wear the non-existent emperor's robe of Fianna Fáil. Mr Lemass is at best mediocre. He is Minister for Industry but we cannot remember any advantage his work has been. Some time recently we saw in the *Sunday Press* a series of profiles of Mr Lemass holding his spectacles in various poses of profundity. We had to laugh. The lighting only exposed the man's shallowness. Of course he isn't any shallower than his companions.'

K: 'It isn't my point of view.'

C: 'You used an expression there and you object to the same expression being used about you.'

K: 'The context is everything. The mood is everything.'

C: 'Those politicians you speak about. Do you accept them all as being ignorant of the subjects they are talking about? Don't you?'

K: 'That is a different thing. It is a very special matter. It doesn't involve a man's livelihood.'

C: 'It might involve the politician's livelihood.'

K: 'It is a public matter … the word shallow on its own is not a harmful word. It is true of most people.'

Quoting once more from the same article, Costello went on: '"The horrible truth is that the level of awareness is much lower here than it is in England as anyone who compares the popular newspapers of both countries will see or anyone who compares the entertainment sent out by the Irish and British radios … All the mouthpieces of public opinion are controlled by men whose only qualification is their inability to think." Is not this passage a comprehensive denunciation of the country's newspapers, Radio Éireann and every other method by which public opinion is formed?'

K: 'That was very serious criticism.'

C: 'I am suggesting that it was a very strong piece of criticism.'

K: 'No. Not from the level at which it was aimed – that was on the heights.'

C: 'The Olympian heights?'

K: 'Yes. That was detached from personalities.'

C: 'Is there anyone but yourself on these heights?'

K: 'You can go there yourself if you wish.'

Laughter in the courtroom.

C: 'Were you detached from personalities when you laughed at Mr Lemass?'

K: 'I do not fully agree with the point of view of that editorial.'

C: 'You were the editor. It was written by you, wasn't it? Didn't you read it?'

K: 'There were at least two paragraphs not written by me.'

C: 'Did you or did you not write that comment upon politicians and upon Mr Lemass in particular?'

K: 'No, not as it appears there. It was changed on the stone in the course of printing.'

Kavanagh went on to explain: 'The thing was done at such terrible speed and I was writing so much, that I never even saw the issue after it was printed. I was looking for adverts which I could not get. I was trying to sell the paper. I was writing a lot of it, eight or nine thousand words a week. The man on the stone in trying to make the article fill the page would put in bits here and there and sometimes impose his own political views on it.'

C: 'Do I gather you are repudiating it or not?'

K: 'I can only tell the truth. It appeared to be so anti-Fianna Fáil.'

C: 'Did you or did you not write the article?'

K: 'I wrote the gist of it. But not the final angle … It was the views of *Kavanagh's Weekly* certainly, but not my personal views.'

Costello mentioned another article from the first issue of the *Weekly*, 'Diplomatic Whiskey': 'Some extraordinary harsh things were said about Ireland's public representatives abroad in that article.'

'I did not write it,' Kavanagh replied.

'I do not care whether you did or not. That came out as part of *Kavanagh's Weekly*.'

'I did not own the *Weekly*.'

Mr Connolly, counsel for Kavanagh, stated that Mr Costello should accept the plaintiff's statement that he had not written it.

C: 'I take it, that you, as editor of the paper, took responsibility for what went into *Kavanagh's Weekly*, the same as any other editor?'

Kavanagh accepted that the article 'Diplomatic Whiskey' had appeared in the *Weekly*.

C: 'Here is something that is there. You are speaking about the waste of time it is for this country to have representatives abroad.'

K: '*Kavanagh's Weekly* is.'

Costello said that the article, referring to the waste of having Irish embassies abroad, said that Irish government representatives abroad in America were hardly ever invited to parties other than to such functions as Galwaymen's dances and that they went in to their offices about ten or eleven in the morning, killed the day as best they could and left at about four or five in the afternoon, going home to their families to drink whiskey and play canasta.

'Was that not a very strong thing to say about our representatives abroad?' asked Costello.

'I know nothing about that,' said Kavanagh. 'I was not entirely responsible for *Kavanagh's Weekly*.'

Costello read: 'The editor of the *Sunday Press* is a military man who has a deep devotion to his führer. We have seen him on a political platform; kiss the edge of an imaginary sword as he named – the Chief!'

Kavanagh agreed that he wrote it, most of it anyway. As he explained: 'When it was being corrected and put on the stone, the man who was doing the job on it or his assistant, I occasionally found he had twisted it to the Fine Gael side.'

Costello responded: 'You did not twist it to my side. You did not say anything about me.' Laughter greeted his response.

Continuing to quote, Mr Costello read: '*The Irish Times* also supported the budget. From different material, but not dissimilar causes, *The Irish Times'* influence has been steadily waning. Without ourselves claiming infallibility, we can say that *The Irish Times* has been for a few years now on the side of the dullest, deadest element in the country. Because it is dull, so many people are inclined to imagine it sound. This doesn't happen. Truth is the gayest of things, and since Myles na gCopaleen left there has been no laughter in *The Irish Times*. Its Saturday book page is a square of flooring timber that would if usable advance any building scheme. Strip the mask of dullness from other contributors and you find vacuity. But we don't want to be derogatory to *The Irish Times* or any other newspaper *per se*. If you choose to patronise the tenants of the intellectual graveyard, it is, in the end, your misfortune.'

Kavanagh accepted that he wrote it: 'I was criticising the literature – or journalism anyway – as I was perfectly entitled to do.'

Asked if he had written the article in which 'The Four Pillars of Wisdom' were designated as the Christian Brothers, Croke Park, Radio Éireann and the Queen's Theatre (the Abbey Theatre), he said he had not.

From the same issue, Costello quoted the passage: '"We would like to see published annually the bank accounts and investments of all our public men and patriots. This would give us an idea of the intention that inspired these men, how far it was selfless, and how far it had to do with the feathering of nests." That was a pretty hot comment on men giving their services to the state. You would require the bank accounts to be produced.'

'I think it is quite fair,' returned Kavanagh. 'It is written in the rhetorical manner. It does not mean to say that I thought everybody should go down and ask to look at their bank accounts.'

Kavanagh agreed he had written a piece in response to the *Sunday Press*: 'Last week the *Sunday Press* attempted to paw us with its flabby hands. This paper, which is modelled on *The News of the World*, *The People*, etc. – what Mr Attlee has called "the most prostituted press in the world" – has the obscene presumption to try to answer us back. The *Sunday Press* is of interest because it is the first Irish paper that has tried to impose on Irish society an alien vulgarity.'

He agreed that in the same issue Radio Éireann had been attacked under the heading, 'The National Bucklep'. He did not write the article although the title was an invention of his. When further questions were put to him shortly before 4 p.m. the witness said: 'I am very tired at the moment. You are taking the thing down to a very low level.'

'We will finish this and then we will let you off,' Costello promised.

The court was adjourned until the following day. Costello had continued to grind away at Kavanagh, alternating between quotes from the profile and from Kavanagh's own writing, comparing and contrasting those. He had also stitched into the record that Kavanagh may have preferred London to Dublin, hardly a legal point but useful for the defence in front of a Dublin-based jury. Costello had tried to hold the plaintiff responsible as editor for all articles published in *Kavanagh's Weekly*.

There was a humorous undertone to Costello, himself a politician, questioning Kavanagh over his allegation that politicians were either shallow or foolish. Not only that, he had then upbraided Kavanagh over his attack on Seán Lemass, a Fianna Fáil minister and a leading opponent of John A. Costello's Fine Gael.

The biggest reaction he had got in the cross-examination to his continuous goading of the witness came when Brendan Behan's name was mentioned. Kavanagh's vehement antipathy to Behan seemed to surprise even Costello. It was a subject he was to revisit. According to John Ryan, Brendan Behan himself, 'who felt that he must, somehow, get in on the act', approached him to ask if Kavanagh would allow him to give evidence on his behalf. 'This offer was rejected with a great show of feeling …'[5]

As Ulick O'Connor, Behan's biographer stated, it was this trial that first made the antagonism between Behan and Kavanagh known to the general public.[6] It stretches credulity that Behan, despite his well-known volatility and his love of the limelight, would care more about getting involved in the case than about which side he would be on.

As Anthony Cronin, a friend of both of the writers portrayed it: 'Costello, quietly and without apparent relevance asked him if he was a friend of Brendan Behan's. The object at that stage may only have been to associate him with somebody disreputable. No harm would have been done if Paddy had replied noncommittally, or casually or even declared that he was unfortunately acquainted with the said party. Instead he grew almost hysterical. In high and passionate tones he described Behan as a low blackguard …' Cronin met Brendan Behan outside the packed courtroom: 'He had a heavy growth of beard, the blue suit was even more crumpled and stained than usual and the open-necked shirt was torn down the front … He was also evidently drunk.'

Cronin was surprised to see him there on the fourth day of the proceedings. Behan shouldered his way through a knot of people towards the outer door and towards where Cronin was standing. Cronin thought he was going to say something significant but he did no more than mutter something about the Monaghan bogman as he passed.[7]

As the case continued, Costello received a letter from Brendan's brother. Seamus wrote from Cootehill, County Cavan:

> Having read this morning's account of the libel case involving Mr Kavanagh, I wish to state that Mr Kavanagh has perjured himself as regards his evidence re. Brendan Behan, my brother. I have frequently seen Mr Kavanagh in my brother's company and I have been myself introduced to Mr Kavanagh by my brother in McDaid's of Grafton Street (Harry St). You may make what use you wish of this letter. I am employed in Cavan but will be in Dublin at the address below from 6 p.m. on Friday 12 February. Any reply may be sent to my Dublin address, 36 Cloyne Road, Kimmage.[8]

It had been another good day for the defence.

Chapter 14

'The horror of his acquaintanceship'

The pressure was beginning to tell on Patrick: the stress of being in the witness box, of, as he saw it, having to account for his life, justifying himself in front of a jury of strangers. Many of his friends noticed how it affected him. John Ryan was particularly concerned: 'If youth had expired with *Kavanagh's Weekly*, old age would set in before this trial finally ended.'[1]

Kavanagh's cross-examination continued. Costello declared that he would like to go back over two matters he raised the previous day, one of which he had overlooked and the other on which he had no certain information at the time.

'I think I diverted you,' Justice Teevan said.

'No, it was through pure oversight.' Costello began with a question with regard to a reference to Lady Cunard in the profile: 'Do you know that Lady Cunard is a patroness of the arts and literature in London literary circles?'

K: 'Yes, I have heard of it.'

C: 'You have criticised the works of Yeats from time to time. Have you read the biography by Holmes of Yeats? Do you know that Lady Cunard has compiled an anthology of works on poetry?'

K: 'I never heard of it.'

C: 'Do you know that Yeats' play *Hawk's Well* was first produced in Lady Cunard's drawing-room in London?'

K: 'No.'

C: 'At all events, is it true that she is a well-known literary patroness?'

K: 'It is not true.'

C: 'I thought you said she was.'

K: 'I am telling you that I heard that but I am telling you I have been in London and she is not. Nobody I know has ever met her.'

C: 'You have criticised Yeats' poems, works and life, and you tell me you did not read Holmes' book on it?'

K: 'No.'

C: 'Therefore you did not see the reference to Lady Cunard in it?'

K: 'How could I see it when I did not read it?'

C: 'You said yesterday rather emphatically that Brendan Behan was never a friend of yours and that he merely painted your flat and you paid him for it?'

K: 'That is correct.'

Costello produced a book that he handed to Kavanagh. 'Isn't that your handwriting on it?' Costello read out: 'For Brendan, poet and painter, on the day he decorated my flat, Sunday 12th, 1950.' He asked again: 'Is that your handwriting?' and added: 'Did you write that to your friend, Brendan?'

'That is my handwriting, surely,' replied Kavanagh. 'I have

been weak on many occasions, and have given my books and written my name ...'

Costello began to ask another follow-up question. Connolly intervened: 'Allow him to finish. This is very unfair. I must protest.'

'That is my handwriting,' Kavanagh admitted. 'People have come to me and cajoled me and it is all right. I was cajoled into doing that for people and one of the reasons I did it was that that man was so offensive every time he met me in the street. That is the only acquaintance that man had with me, that every time he met me in the street he shouted at me in not very nice language. He shouted at me everywhere, and in my efforts to get rid of that attack I have not only – I have many times been friendly to him, hoping that I would be free from the horror of his acquaintanceship, and that – it is something horrible to me. I am terrified of him. I did all kinds of things, but I will do anything – I sincerely say, I do not wish – I want to be truly sincere about that. I hate to say anything really cruel, but there is something always in that man that, to my mind, was not good, and I did that purely to, you know – you do that to somebody, you would even praise them, hoping that they will leave you alone, my Lord, and I have done that in my work again and again, hoping that I would get rid of it and get rid of him.' The normally composed and articulate Kavanagh was for once stuck for words, perhaps a sign of the stress he was under by this stage.

Costello was unmoved: 'The jury may take it that you presented to Brendan Behan a copy of your work with this inscription: "For Brendan, poet and painter, on the day he decorated my flat, Sunday 12th, 1950", and that you autographed it, Patrick Kavanagh?'

Connolly interjected: 'And Brendan presented it to *The Leader*.'

'Brendan did not present it to *The Leader*. I want to get that remark withdrawn. Brendan did not present that to *The Leader* at all,' argued Costello. 'I had not this information yesterday, nor did I anticipate from the instructions I had that the denial given by Mr Kavanagh in the box would have been given in the manner it was given. I only got the information on this morning.'

Addressing the witness Justice Teevan said that all Mr Costello wanted to know was whether he had given the autographed copy of the book to Mr Behan.

'I did.'

'On the day he decorated your flat?' Costello inquired.

'I must say this in the cause of justice, my Lord … I gave my books to many people, and deeply regret I found their characters afterwards,' Kavanagh replied.

'You can be re-examined on this by your own counsel,' Justice Teevan advised.

C: 'Do I understand from your last statement that you found out something about him after you had given him the presentation copy?'

K: 'Yes.'

C: 'May I recall what you said yesterday, that Behan never was a friend of yours?'

K: 'I say that again. I even praised him to himself hoping that by doing so I would somehow lessen the evil that I believed was in him. He was never a friend of mine.'

C: 'You suggested yesterday that he was on the same par or level as the plumber who did the plumbing in your house.'

'Oh, no he didn't,' Justice Teevan intervened, 'that is a misinterpretation. You suggested that he should be acquainted with Behan, and he said he knew the name of his plumber.'

Costello rephrased: 'When you said yesterday that Mr Smith had done the plumbing and you knew Mr Smith, that, I suggest, was intended to convey that Mr Behan was on the same par as Mr Smith – a casual tradesman doing work in your flat.'

'He was very nearly on the same par, not quite on the same par but very nearly,' replied Kavanagh. 'He was on the same par, as a matter of fact. I said that for flattery.'

Costello finally moved away from the topic of his fraught relationship with Behan. Kavanagh wanted to say more but the judge told him firmly that he must only answer questions put to him.

Costello returned to *Kavanagh's Weekly* and some comments that had been made about eminent people and institutions of the country: 'I want to give you some more quotations,' he warned.

In *Kavanagh's Weekly* it had been written that 'the army and navy are always referred to by government officials as our defence forces, although what they could possibly defend the country against is a problem we have not worked out. They would certainly be good at defending a field of turnips against an invasion of crows. At present they are defending themselves against the prospect of doing any constructive work – at least as far as the officers are concerned, it is a professional conspiracy against the common man. Being an officer is a cushy job and that is about the sum total of patriotism.'

'Have you any comment to make on that?' asked Costello.

'I did not write it,' Kavanagh replied.

'As editor, aren't you responsible for everything that appears in the *Weekly*?' reminded Costello.

'No,' said Kavanagh and added, 'I said something yesterday I want to clear up. All leaders were written by me but whenever my brother got a chance he did his best to put forward his own point of view. Any time I saw it I tried to cut his point of view out.'

Kavanagh repudiated his brother's views and added: 'I can defend my viewpoint against anybody.'

'I am not suggesting it is your point of view,' Costello stated. He then quoted from an article in the *Weekly* called 'The Threepence on the Pint': 'It is hard to say what Conradh na Gaedhilge is, but I find they are listed in the telephone directory as having an office in Dublin. Whatever they are, they are a smart crowd, but they are lying very low.' And then from further down in the article: '"The Folklore Commission collects dust in St Stephen's Green." Do you know the Folklore Commission?'

Mr Connolly intervened: 'The article, according to the evidence was not written by Mr Kavanagh. I submit that my friend, if he can do so, can do no more than put the article [before the court].'

Justice Teevan agreed. He told Costello, 'you are only entitled to put up the fact. You cannot cross-examine the witness on it.'

Undeterred Costello resumed his readings from *Kavanagh's*

Weekly: 'The Institute for Advanced Studies gets £62,830. This is a child of de Valera's pet vanity – physics. There are no regular students and apparently nothing for the professors to do. I visited the institute on Monday evening. It must have been pay-day because I could hear roars of laughter coming from every room.'

Costello paused to let the quotation sink in, then recommenced: 'The Irish News Agency, with offices in the basement of Irish Shell House, Fleet St, Dublin, gets £25,000 a year.'

Costello went on to quote from an attack on the cost of running Radio Éireann and then moved on to the Cultural Relations Committee: 'The Cultural Relations Committee which gets £10,000 a year, has been treated in a previous issue of the journal. It is run by the Department of External Affairs and one of its main functions is to send certain people to obscure places on the map to lecture on the glorious heritage of Gaelic culture. We have been told how one man was sent to lecture to the Eskimos.

'The Arts Council, recently established is to get £10,000 a year. The chairman is Mr Patrick Little, ex-Minister for Posts and Telegraphs. The money will, no doubt be spent nice and quietly.'

Those that had served in 1916 also came in for a mention: '£166,496 is paid out annually to the persons who served in 1916. In 1951 there were 1,336 such persons, in 1952 the number rose to 1,702 persons and, no doubt, next year it will go up again. The word "served" is very useful because it has so many meanings. Considering the number who have died since

1916 and the number now drawing pensions, they must have been a poor lot to have capitulated so quickly.'

Kavanagh pointed out that he had not written that article.

'THE CONFUSERS MUST BE CONFOUNDED'

Costello said that in one issue of *Kavanagh's Weekly*, a lecture that the witness had given in UCD was reproduced in which it was stated:

> During the past fifty years there had been two men of high talent and perhaps genius in this country – Yeats and Joyce. One has only to do a superficial study to see the treatment Irish society gave to these two. Yet, the barbarism of Irish society has a merit in this regard; a requisite in the making of a profound artist. Yeats owes in this way a good deal to Ireland, and now that he is dead we might ever regret that he did not suffer enough from Irish barbarism … Joyce, on the other hand, got all that Ireland had to give him, and his reaction to it made him great …
>
> … the architect does not suffer too much from this kind of barbarous society; for the architect's profession is dumb, except in exceptional circumstances. The Irish tradition is only worried about men who might tell the truth; and you can hardly tell much of either truth or lies through the medium of concrete. The same applies to painting and music. Absolute truth is met with absolute hate. So, in Ireland, the only person who is likely to suffer till the heart is turned to stone is the writer – when such an animal happens to appear.
>
> At the same time, I must admit that I do find, and we have found since starting a weekly paper, that there is a considerable

public of generous-minded people who realise the futility of materialism. But before this minority can become in any way powerful the confusers must be confounded. The Arts Council and the Cultural Relations Committee, and the men who hold wireless symposiums on the problem of the writer in Ireland, must be killed off or there is no chance. What makes them so hard to get at is that they look like friends.

'What makes them so hard to get at is that they look like friends?' Costello asked.

'Precisely,' Kavanagh replied.

An article in the *Weekly* was referred to in which it was suggested that there was a shortage of goats in Ireland causing difficulty for the Puck Fair in Killorglin: 'This is a problem which might engage the attention of Mr P.J. Little's Arts Council. After all, he could spend the £10,000 a year government grant on many things of less interest.'

Next under scrutiny was an editorial from the second last issue of the paper titled 'Freedom How Are Ye!': 'As it is, the power of the Christian ethic is getting less and less. This is almost more true of Ireland than of several other countries which make no pretence of being Christian. Money talks everywhere, but in Ireland nothing else talks. Freedom of speech, freedom of the Press – a joke.'

Having established his case, at length, Costello asked: 'Would it be correct for me to say that, because of the views you held – perhaps sincerely held on various matters of literature and Radio Éireann – it was impossible for you in the years before starting *Kavanagh's Weekly* to get employment in any of the newspapers or publications in Dublin?'

K: 'I have been writing for every paper in Dublin since I came to the city in 1939 and the problem with me was that I never was able to keep up with the demand. More people have written to me for my work than I ever was able to supply.'

C: 'I am just going to test that now. Radio Éireann – you had not taken part there for years before this started?'

K: 'No, but they wrote to me just the same. I was asked by Francis MacManus to contribute but I did not reply.'

C: 'By reason of the views you held about Radio Éireann, you did not broadcast for them?'

K: 'I was not interested in them, and apart from that, I would not be very well paid either.'

C: 'Which?'

K: 'I am not really interested in radio as a medium.'

C: 'I thought it was put that you were.'

K: 'I did a bit of it. I am interested in it to make money. It is a good way of making money … I have a point of view and I am glad to put it forward anywhere, with or without money. I always had the same point of view. I have it today … It is a truthful one.'

C: 'Would it be true to say that there are vast numbers of people who do not agree with it?'

'There is at the moment a small pernicious minority and you represent it,' Kavanagh retorted, then immediately apologised. 'Is that wrong? I am sorry to say that, I am very sorry.'

'Ah, Mr Kavanagh, I don't mind,' Costello said.

'I am very sorry to say that,' repeated Kavanagh.

'I am sure you didn't mean offence,' Justice Teevan comforted him.

'I took no offence at it, Mr Kavanagh. All I want to get from you are the facts,' Costello assured him, before returning to the attack. 'Radio Éireann, if they wanted to, could not employ you with the views you held.'

K: 'Indeed they would and would be quite glad to get me … These people do not care what you say about them. If you are a good man they will employ you and be pleased to do so.'

C: 'The fact is that, in the years before 1952, you were not employed, whatever the reason, by Radio Éireann.'

K: 'I did not want to be employed. They did not pay very well. The BBC wanted me to speak verse. I was told that I was one of the best speakers of verse they had ever heard.'

'Radio Éireann?' Mr Justice Teevan asked.

K: 'No, the BBC, to read a book. Of course I agreed with them.'

C: 'However, the fact remains that from 1949 to 1952 little or nothing of your work appeared in the Irish newspapers.'

K: 'I was too busy then. In that period I wrote three novels. I would like to say that if I wanted to write, I could write.'

The judge intervened: 'Would you agree that little or no work appeared in the papers over the period 1949 to 1952?'

K: 'I would say there was no difference between it generally and any other period. As a freelance journalist it is immaterial to me where I publish my work.'

C: 'In 1947 and 1948, you did not contribute one signed article to *The Irish Times* Saturday literary page.'

K: 'I did not. They would love to get me, just the same.'

C: 'From 1949 to 1952, you had nothing in *The Irish Times* either.'

K: 'I contributed no signed articles but a lot of articles appeared in *The Irish Times* under pseudonyms.'

C: 'Do you agree with me that from 1947 to 1952 you did not contribute anything, or anything of consequence, to *The Irish Times*?'

K: 'I have other jobs to do besides writing for *The Irish Times*.'

C: 'Do you agree with me that that is the fact?'

K: 'It probably is.'

C: 'Did you contribute to the *Irish Independent*?'

K: 'I have not contributed to the *Irish Independent* for years. I never sent them anything.'

Mr Connolly pointed out that, there being no reference in the profile to the *Irish Independent*, no question of libel therefore arose in regards to them.

Kavanagh agreed that he had been retained as a staff journalist by the *Standard* for a time.

'I want to suggest again that, because of your strong views on various matters, however sincerely held, and because of your attacks on journalism, the newspapers were not anxious to employ you,' Costello continued.

'You are quite wrong,' replied Kavanagh.

Costello proceeded to read from an article from *Envoy* dated January 1950 in which Kavanagh had written: 'As one who had engaged in journalism, nothing amuses me more ironically than to see newspapers accusing one another, thereby implying a standard of ethics amongst newspapers. A group of newspapers accusing one another thus are like a group of fag-pulling ladies-in-waiting on O'Connell Street at 1 a.m. moralising. Fundamentally there is no difference between a newspaper which calls itself Catholic and the one which makes plain dirt its theme.'

Costello continued to select excerpts from this article, in which Kavanagh stated that the main aspect of popular journalism was a knowledge of crosswords, the use of vulgar slang words such as 'teenage' and abbreviations such as 'congrats': 'All contributors to a popular paper should have a silly face, which would be placed at the top of a column. Popular newspapers should be written "by the office boy for office boys". This was the Northcliffe theory and practice. There were a number of intelligent men in Dublin journalism but they had no chance.'

Kavanagh spoke in his defence: 'I meant that intelligent journalists have no chance to put forward their points of view. There was certainly a chance for a man with strong views on other matters to get employment on Dublin newspapers. The trouble with the newspaper generally is that it takes in both truth and falsehood. Its articles are mutually destructive.'

C: 'Your view is that it would be difficult for a writer like you to make a living in Ireland?'

K: 'It is difficult for a writer to make a living at all. It is difficult for a man who tells the truth. If I really told the truth they would take me up on a high hill and crucify me.'

C: 'That is the point. You are the preacher of absolute truth. You could not be employed by the popular newspapers of which you are complaining.'

K: 'I do not agree. If I had sent the articles which I wrote for *Kavanagh's Weekly* to any of these newspapers, they would have printed them, and then, instead of losing several hundred pounds on *Kavanagh's Weekly*, we would have made a lot of money. As it was, they were given to the country for nothing.'

C: 'With regard to *Kavanagh's Weekly*, your brother Peter called the tune?'

K: 'Largely. He did his best to call the tune.'

C: 'You pretty well did what he told you to do.'

K: 'Not quite. As I explained earlier I wrote most of the paper. Every time he got a chance, he inserted his point of view, as most men try to do. Every time I saw his point of view in it, and had time, I cut it out.'

C: 'As a preacher of the ultimate truth, you must have been irked a bit by these conditions imposed by your brother?'

K: 'He did not impose any conditions. He just did his best. I don't mind what he wrote himself, but every now and again I didn't always agree with a word he put in because it changed the texture of the article which I did not always see.'

Returning to *The Leader* article, Costello said: 'In various phrases you have been throwing around you have talked about "taking the dinner off your plate", suggesting that the writer of the profile was responsible for this.'

'I am saying it was an attempt to ruin me and destroy my influence,' replied Kavanagh.

'Far from having this effect,' Costello alleged, 'you have earned more money in Dublin since the profile was written than you had for many previous years.'

K: 'Indeed I have not.'

C: 'I suggest you have been employed by Radio Éireann in the last few years far more times than for years before.'

K: 'The only reason I am going on Radio Éireann is because they have a new director there, Mr Maurice Gorham.'

Asked what had become of the contract he had with Macmillan (the publishers of *Ploughman and Other Poems* in 1936 and *A Soul for Sale* in 1947), Kavanagh said: 'I have written books and they will be published.'

C: 'Was that broken by Macmillans because you were not carrying it out?'

K: 'No.'

C: 'Did you contribute to Macmillans from 1947 until the present moment, February 1954, one single piece of writing?'

K: 'I have written it. It will go on in due course. Imagination does not go by a time; it might be five years as a matter of fact.'

Pressed further on this point, Kavanagh said he had not handed in the work yet; they were waiting for it and he was going to submit it. He also denied that he had been drawing £300 a year under the contract for doing nothing.

C: 'Yet you have not submitted a manuscript since 1948?'

K: 'I did not do so. I did not think it good enough.'

C: 'So Macmillans are getting no return?'

K: 'They are getting it every day from the copyright of my works … They know I am a good mark and I'll produce the stuff for them and I am also prestige value and that is what they want.'

C: 'I have not heard of publishers paying in advance for prestige value.'

K: 'Of course they do. Macmillans lost a fortune on Yeats' books. It was prestige entirely. All publishers subsidise for prestige.'

Costello then made reference to an advertisement the previous evening offering a bound set of *Kavanagh's Weekly* for 100 guineas saying: 'That rather shows that as a result of this action your stock has gone up', to which Kavanagh replied: 'I do not agree. I did not put it in. I know nothing about it.'

'I am not suggesting you did for a moment,' said Costello. 'Somebody thinks they will get a 100 guineas or more.'

'Someone who doesn't like us put that in,' retorted Kavanagh.

Costello then moved on to the matter of an article in *The Bell* written by The Bellman (Larry Morrow) and entitled 'Meet Mr Kavanagh', which appeared in 1948. As the witness had claimed that the profile in *The Leader* had ridiculed him and made him out to be a buffoon, Costello wanted to quote from this piece in which the plaintiff was described as 'a stage Irishman about town'. Costello said to Kavanagh: 'You did not object to this?'

'It was humorous,' Kavanagh responded. 'The mood of humour is all through it. That took all the evil out of it.'

Kavanagh went on to tell that court: 'A similar article with a slightly different angle also written by Larry Morrow appeared in the *Sunday Empire News* about four years later. I contacted the Dublin editor of the *Sunday Empire News*, Sam Edgar, that I know.' When Kavanagh rang the editor of the *Sunday Empire News* the editor said: '"I know it is a libel on Kavanagh; I know that profile is libel." It shows you how the angle shifts.'

Kavanagh stated that he had, in that instance, complained about the *Sunday Empire News* and in response, 'the editor offered me a good fee to write an article in reply'.

Undeterred Costello continued quoting from Morrow's article: 'The work also states that if Mr Kavanagh "wrote anonymous letters to himself and believed them to come from someone else I would not be surprised."'

Connolly objected on the grounds that this was irrelevant. Costello disagreed: 'It is relevant on his evidence. He says that we held him up to ridicule and buffoonery. This made him a source of buffoonery.'

Mr Justice Teevan ruled that it may have relevance with regard to the question of mitigation of damages. Now that had been clarified, Costello returned to The Bellman and *The Bell*. He read to the jury that Mr Kavanagh 'shares with Mr Frank Sinatra, Dylan Thomas, Picasso and the Marx Brothers the capacity for arousing the emotions to the screaming point either for or against him.'

Costello further quoted The Bellman, who called Kavanagh 'a broth of a boy' and said he had a 'great root-like hand' that cast a shadow on a café table. He continued, saying that Mr Kavanagh was quoted in the article as saying: 'I've been telling lies all my life.' It is stated that 'nuclear fission is a ripple in a tea cup compared with Mr Kavanagh in a tea shop' and in reference to the poet's teeth that 'it would be a poor vet who could not tell Mr Kavanagh's age from them'.

As to the article in *The Leader* Costello asked Kavanagh if he was aware that the profile was one of a series of anonymously written articles? Kavanagh stated that he had heard about the articles but knew nothing about them all being anonymous. Costello returned to the first letter written by the plaintiff's solicitors to *The Leader*.

'At least ten days after you saw the article?' Costello asked. 'It was ten days before you went to see your solicitor?'

He replied: 'I was very disturbed and wondered if there was any justice in the world that could answer that horrible thing. That was one worry on me.'

'The question was only asked about the length of time,' the judge pointed out.

'I would say a couple of days,' Kavanagh explained. 'I was in London when the article appeared. A copy of it was sent to me by a friend, a friend who was incapable of commenting.'

Asked why particular grounds of complaint were not mentioned in his solicitor's letters to *The Leader,* Kavanagh replied: 'It is easy to see what is in it – the total assassination of character. The total.'

Costello asked Kavanagh why the exchange of letters between the solicitors had been described as 'fruitless correspondence'?

K: 'Fruitless dealing with the devil.'

C: 'Would I be right in describing you as dive-bombing *The Leader* to get compensation?'

K: 'Dive-bombing? What do you mean? What am I to say?'

C: 'You had the writ out before you could receive a letter from our solicitors. While our solicitors were writing a reply, your solicitors were down here in court taking out a summons.'

K: 'Anyone who looks at the article knows very well that while I expect to get substantial damages, that it is by no means my main purpose.' Kavanagh went on: 'In asking me for particulars of my complaint you have the objective of wearing me down, as in the past three days here. The object was to wear me down and destroy me.'

C: 'What about the *Sunday Empire News*? Did you threaten them with a libel action?'

K: 'I did not. I rang up Sam Edgar in Dublin and said I did not like the article and he said that the editor of the *Sunday Empire News* said it was a serious thing and said he would pay me a good fee for writing another article in reply.'

C: 'He gave you space to reply?'

K: 'Yes, because I did not approve of going to law.'

C: 'Why did you not give *The Leader* the same chance you had given the *Empire News*, namely to write an article in reply to the profile?'

K: 'I would not be evil enough to answer that article. Nobody could do it. Only the pen of some man who had been down in hell could have written it.'

C: 'You did not give *The Leader* – an Irish newspaper that has been in existence for fifty years – the same chance as you gave to the British paper.'

'That is strychnine, dosed with strychnine,' Kavanagh answered. 'That is poisonous.'

Costello's cross-examination of Kavanagh ended on this toxic note. The court then adjourned for lunch.

'MY PRESENT MIND IS TERRIBLE'

Next up for Kavanagh was cross-examination by Mr Fitzgerald for Argus, the printers of *The Leader*. However, when the judge took his seat on the bench at 2 p.m. after the lunch interval, Kavanagh was not in his usual place. The session was delayed for thirty minutes because Kavanagh was, in the words of his counsel, 'overwrought' after a 'very severe ordeal over a number of days'. Connolly told the judge: 'Mr Kavanagh was quite unwell, my Lord and he is in a room outside the court. Would you mind delaying the cross-examination by Mr Fitzgerald?'

'He should be given an opportunity of recovering,' Fitzgerald stated, 'it would be undesirable that another witness be interposed.'

The court adjourned for a further fifteen minutes and Kavanagh re-entered the witness box having been examined by Doctor H. Hession from Rooskey, Dromod, County Leitrim, who was in the High Court as a witness in another case.[2] He was of the opinion that it would be more preferable to finish the cross-examination than to have it deferred for another day.

Back in the witness box Kavanagh held his head in his hands and answered only in a low whisper. After John A. Costello's impressive tour de force and his methodical dismantling of Kavanagh over three days, it was Mr Fitzgerald's turn to earn his fee.

To ease the disconsolate witness, he started off with a philosophical question: 'I would like to have your views as an author and writer on whether you approve or disapprove of state censorship, that is, restriction being imposed by the state on what people may or may not write or publish.'

Kavanagh: 'I think there has to be censorship of some kind. My belief is that only that which is good has an impact, and I believe that which is evil really does less damage ... I do think, in a way, that I agree with some of it, anyway, to some extent.'

Fitzgerald: 'I was not asking for your reasons. If you don't understand the question say so. I would have thought that any writer would have a strong view one way or the other. Do I gather from you that you think it is a good thing that the state should have a power of censorship – but limited?'

K: 'I think it is essential that bad stuff should be kept out anyway.'

F: 'Would you agree, granted adequate state censorship, in the sense you say is desirable, that commercial printers should not seek to exercise an unofficial censorship by declining to publish material which is all right from the state censorship point of view?'

K: 'They printed it.'

F: 'That is not the question I asked.'

K: 'It is their duty, in my opinion, to act as censors.'

F: 'It is your view that commercial printers should also act as censors apart from any state censorship?'

K: 'Generally speaking they do.'

'If the action lies in law,' Connolly said, 'I submit that Mr Kavanagh's opinion on the subject is quite irrelevant.'

Fitzgerald argued that it was relevant to Mr Kavanagh's credibility as to why he had brought the action against a commercial printer.

Justice Teevan agreed with Connolly: 'If the law permits an action for libel against printers it is the duty of the printer to exclude libel. I will rule it out.'

Fitzgerald moved on to the question of motivation: 'Now, Mr Kavanagh in this action, as originally constituted, you had as defendants, *The Leader*, Messrs Argus whom you now accept had no venom against you, and Messrs Eason's whom I suppose you also regarded as having no venom against you, and who dealt with it as a commercial transaction?'

K: 'Yes.'

F: 'Would I be right in thinking that your purpose in joining my clients Argus and Eason's was to get, if you succeed in getting a verdict, the substantial damages out of their pockets in case *The Leader* could not pay?'

K: 'I just told my solicitors. I don't know.'

F: 'Listen to me. I am putting it to you that your purpose in joining the two people who had no venom against you was to ensure that if you do get substantial damages and *The Leader* could not pay it, that you would be able to take it off one or either of the other defendants who had no venom against you?'

K: 'I did not know who printed the article when I wrote to my solicitor.'

F: 'You learned it quickly.'

K: 'A long time afterwards.'

F: 'You know now.'

K: 'I do, yes.'

Fitzgerald then quoted two letters written by the plaintiff's solicitors – one to the proprietors of *The Leader* and the other to the proprietors of Argus Ltd. He pointed out that in the letter to *The Leader*, the plaintiff sought an unreserved apology, the name of the author of the article and substantial compensation. Whereas, all that was required of Argus was substantial damages: 'You did not ask for or suggest an apology from Argus? Your sole demand was for money. Do you observe that?'

'It is a solicitor's letter,' Kavanagh replied.

F: 'Don't mind whose it is for the moment. Do you observe that to my clients there is no suggestion that you want an apology? What you wanted was money?'

K: 'An apology is very important.'

F: 'But the demand is for money and nothing else, no demand for the name of the author, just a demand for money. Isn't that so?'

K: 'I cannot help it. It is a solicitor's letter.'

F: 'On your instructions?'

K: 'I could not tell my solicitor what to do. How would I know? I just tell him the facts of the case. He can do what he likes.'

F: 'You would have been satisfied apparently, to get an apology, the name of the author, and some money from *The Leader* but all you wanted off my clients is money? Is that still so?'

K: 'I don't know anything at all about that.'

Justice Teevan explained: 'Mr Fitzgerald is asking about your present attitude at this very moment.'

K: 'My present mind is terrible. I am not thinking.'

F: 'You will have to think whether all you want from my client is money.'

K: 'If I get compensation, I don't care who it comes from.'

F: 'You don't care whether you get it off the man with the venom against you or the commercial people who did the printing so long as you get it and the law makes them amenable. Is that the position?'

K: 'I am doing my best.'

F: 'You are not addressing yourself to the question. Is your only claim money?'

K: 'I am doing my best.'

F: 'You are not addressing yourself to the question. Is your only claim money? You don't want an apology?'

K: 'I go by the law and what my legal people tell me. I don't know. It never occurred to me.'

F: 'The position in law is that my clients are in exactly the same position – having no venom against you – as anybody who might have venom against you. If it occurs to you as unfair, the remedy lies in your hands – you can get all you require from *The Leader* without dragging in my clients. Do you appreciate that?'

K: 'I have no comment to make.'

F: 'I put it to you that whatever the justification may be in trying to establish your character or teach a lesson to the men who wrote this article about you, that no purpose is being served by having my clients here in this court except your anxiety to make them pay for something that you complain somebody else really did.'

K: 'I just told the solicitor and he did all the rest.'

F: 'Do you stand over it?'

K: 'I have to stand over what the solicitor said.'

F: 'In your case you don't. Are you now in the position

that if you are fortunate enough to get a verdict from the jury for substantial damages that you are going to use the law to get money off my clients although they published it as a commercial proposition?'

K: 'I don't care where it comes from.'

'You don't care where it comes from,' Fitzgerald repeated slowly, 'as long as you get the money. Is that the position?'

Kavanagh disagreed.

F: 'It is no use in shaking your head at me. The note-taker cannot take it down and it does not impress me. Is that the position?'

K: 'I am not so interested. I want redress.'

F: 'What redress are you seeking?'

K: 'Financial compensation and an apology.'

F: 'Are you now asking my clients for an apology?'

K: 'I suppose they should, in a way.'

F: 'I want to know whether you are now suggesting my clients should apologise or not?'

K: 'I would say they should apologise.'

F: 'Do you think they should?'

K: 'Oh, I don't care.'

F: 'I am not asking what you care. I am asking you now whether you now suggest that my clients should apologise.'

K: 'I am only interested in an apology and compensation. I don't know who should apologise.'

F: 'Then you are not suggesting that my client should apologise?'

K: 'Somebody should apologise.'

F: 'You never asked my clients to apologise, did you?'

K: 'I don't know whether my solicitors did or not.'

F: 'Don't you know there was no other letter written to Argus, only the October 18 one – the demand for money?'

K: 'Yes.'

F: 'And your position now is that you want redress and it needs to be money and you don't care who pays?'

K: 'Yes, I suppose so. That would be right.'

F: 'Do you agree it would be rather difficult for authors if commercial printing firms were to discard articles because they did not like them or because there was a possibility of objection being taken to them by solicitors?'

K: 'It would be difficult, I suppose.'

F: 'You yourself would have considerable difficulty in getting a number of your articles printed if the commercial printers took that attitude?'

K: 'Some do.'

F: 'A lot of them do not.'

K: 'Yes.'

F: 'But a lot of them published articles from you highly critical of other people?'

K: 'Yes.'

F: 'You would have been very aggrieved if your publishers said, "I cannot print that because it disparages somebody else".'

K: 'I suppose I would.'

F: 'Do you agree that Argus were entitled to take a more favourable view of the author in not refusing to publish something?'

K: 'I agree.'

F: 'And notwithstanding that, being satisfied my clients had no venom against you because they printed this article, you are prepared to plunge your hand into their pocket?'

Connolly intervened to point out: 'My client is not responsible for the law as my friend suggests.'

'I did not suggest he is responsible,' argued Fitzgerald.

On re-examination Mr Connolly asked Mr Kavanagh if he had any responsibility for the way the action had been brought or if he had left it to his solicitor and counsel.

K: 'I left it entirely in their hands.'

Connolly: 'Does the same apply to the correspondence before the action was brought – the letters written by Mr O'Connor?'

K: 'Yes.'

Connolly: 'As regards the form which these letters took, did you leave the matter to your solicitor?'

K: 'Yes, I left it all to him.'

Connolly: 'Are you aware if there was any reply to the letter written to the printers?'

K: 'I cannot say.'

Connolly: 'In the action as it stands, are you aware that you are claiming damages against the two defendants?'

K: 'Yes.'

Connolly: 'To your knowledge has there been state interference with any publication containing any work of yours with the exception of *Tarry Flynn* which was banned for three days?'

K: 'None of the other books have ever been banned.'

Connolly: 'In the case of *Tarry Flynn*, the ban was lifted after three days?'

K: 'Yes.'

Connolly: 'Whatever references have been made here to obscenity, it has never been the subject of any interference with your works by the authorities?'

K: 'No, they have never done anything like that. The publication *Horizon* was never banned and never seized.'

Connolly: 'You have been asked whether the position was that when you started *Kavanagh's Weekly* you were at that time unable to get contributions of yours into the other Dublin newspapers. Is that true?'

K: 'It is not true. There is no truth whatever in the suggestion that because of the opinions I had expressed that I would not be employed.'

Connolly: 'Did you fall foul of one of those five institutions – *The Irish Times*, the Irish News Agency, the *Standard*, the Department of External Affairs or Radio Éireann – at that time?'

K: 'No.'

Connolly: 'Did anything happen in the case of any one of these five which would justify the statements that they had either lost your services or refrained from calling on them?'

K: 'That is nonsense. It is not true at all.'

Connolly: 'It is suggested that beyond this new magazine *Kavanagh's Weekly* there were no other outlets for your literary efforts. Is that a true representation of your position at the time?'

K: 'No.'

Referring to the profile in *The Leader* Kavanagh was asked: 'Have you any objection to the way the matter in regard to the

Minister of External Affairs refusing to pay your passage to the United States is stated?'

K: 'I have. It is made to convey that I went to the Minister as a beggar.'

Connolly: 'In the case of the writers who have been mentioned here, has there ever been any complaint made to you or the journals to which you contributed about your references to them?'

K: 'Not that I know of.'

Connolly: 'Either as literary criticism or if there is any other personal grounds?'

K: 'There have been controversies.'

Connolly: 'Nothing in the nature of legal proceedings?'

K: 'No.'

Connolly: 'As far as you know, there was nothing in the nature of complaints to the different papers?'

K: 'Not that I know of.'

So concluded the plaintiff's evidence.

An attempt was made to call Professor W.B. Stanford as a character witness for Kavanagh. William Bedell Stanford was a classical scholar and senator. He was Professor of Greek at Trinity College. Costello objected on the grounds that the entire matter for the jury to decide was whether or not the article was defamatory. The opinion of an outside person as to the plaintiff's literary standing could not be given because the plaintiff's standing was not an issue in the case. Fitzgerald for Argus Printers also objected on the grounds that the calling of that evidence would be substituting Professor Stanford's opinion for the opinion of the jury.

Thomas Doyle, for the plaintiff, counter-argued that the jury were entitled to have independent technical evidence of the plaintiff's standing in society and in literature.

Costello replied: 'Far from challenging Mr Kavanagh's standing, on the contrary, we have complimented him in a way he has never been complimented before.'

Mr Justice Teevan ruled that Professor Stanford's evidence was inadmissible.

Peadar O'Toole, an official of the Department of Justice was then called and he gave evidence that there was no record of any Prohibition Order made by the Censorship Board in relation to *Horizon* in 1942. That closed the plaintiff's case.

Costello announced that he did not intend to tender any evidence for the defence. But he would ask the judge to rule, as a matter of law, that the article as a whole was incapable of being defamatory and to rule out the 'so-called innuendos' as being incapable, as a matter of law, of being sustained.

Costello also raised the point that the defence had not disclosed the name of the writer of the article. He cited authority for this stance; on the proposition that it was well established law that, as far as newspapers were concerned, neither by discovery or interrogatories could the name of the writer of an anonymous article be obtained. That rule, he said, did not apply to publications that were not newspapers in the strict sense.

Counsel's addresses to the jury would begin the following morning.

It had been yet another good day for the defence. The Behan episode was what the newspapers would lead with. It was the sensation of the trial that two such eminent literary figures could be carrying on a feud in the streets and pubs of Dublin. As to who had handed over the autographed copy of *Tarry Flynn* to the defence, it is generally believed that it was not Brendan but another member of his family.

According to Ulick O'Connor, Behan's biographer, it was Rory Furlong, Brendan's half-brother who, 'without Brendan's knowledge', had delivered the book into Costello's hands and that 'Brendan was furious with Rory for doing this and told him that he should never interfere between writers.'[3]

While the episode was not a crucial point of the case, it was by far the most sensational and it could, perhaps, affect the jury's attitude to Kavanagh and cast doubt on his credibility and in particular, on his veracity in the witness box.

While it was true that Patrick was under great stress, given the length of time he had spent under cross-examination, it is also possible that the sudden illness was a play for the sympathy of the jury. Peter had suggested such a tactic to his brother. He felt that Costello was going to continue until he broke Kavanagh so the best way to out-flank him was to choose his own moment to crumple.[4]

However, this does not tally with what actually happened. Patrick's 'collapse' happened after the end of Costello's cross-examination, which might lead one to believe it was genuine. If it was going to be staged to disrupt Costello it would have occurred sometime during his questioning, not when it was all over.

The cross-examination of Patrick with regard to censorship and his attitude to printers in general, recalls the difficulty the brothers had locating a printer who was willing to take the risk of printing *Kavanagh's Weekly*. Peter described their troubles:

> My job was to find a printer. This, at first seemed a fairly easy assignment since I was to be a cash customer. But in Dublin printers are not to be bought with the kind of small cash I had on offer. They wanted to know about all sorts of things. Had I a mock-up of the *Weekly*? What was to be its policy? Who were to be the owners? How much money had they, knowing full well they had nothing or close to it? How long will this *Weekly* run? Will we be insured against libel?
>
> After several hours travelling and interviewing I eventually came across a small printer in a cul de sac off Dorset Street. He was trying to get established and needed money badly ... I put down a deposit on the job and a day or two later went back for the proofs ... He had made some cuts in some of the pieces because of libel ...

Peter recalls setting the printer straight: 'If there were to be any changes they would be by the editor. You are merely the printer and if you insist on intruding that is the end of our agreement. He pulled in his horns reluctantly.'[5]

It was in fact the Fleet Printing Company, 6 Eccles Place, that published the thirteen issues of *Kavanagh's Weekly*. The article in the first issue that caused the most apprehension was one written by Peter about the Irish diplomatic service. In retrospect, the wonder is that *Kavanagh's Weekly* did not end up in the courts. Perhaps any prospective plaintiff was put off by the realisation that there would be no money in it.

In later life Peter constructed his own printing press in the basement of his house in New York and published a number of books, many of them on his brother's life and works. As a printer, he was no stranger to the courtroom, copyright law being his particular bugbear.

Chapter 15

'The dull, grey verbal savagery of the law'

On what was expected to be the final day of the case, the opening of proceedings was delayed until after midday because the court was engaged in other routine business. Nevertheless, people determined to get seats in the gallery began arriving at the Four Courts as early as 10.30 a.m. A queue formed in the central hall, marshalled by the ushers.

When the judge took his seat on the bench he said he would read out the questions he intended to put to the jury and then counsel could argue them. The jury then retired and left the legal eagles to it.

Seated in the body of the court, waiting for a call that never came to give evidence, John Ryan had not been impressed by the proceedings: 'Day followed tedious day of crafty innuendo, turgid repartee, the fiction of ignorance and all the dull, grey verbal savagery of the law.'[1]

The judge refused applications by the defence to withdraw the case from the jury on the grounds that the article as a whole was incapable of being defamatory. A long debate then took place as to the exact questions that would be put to the jury.

On resumption after lunch Mr Justice Teevan determined that there would be eight questions:

1. Is the said article as a whole, in its ordinary meaning, defamatory of the plaintiff?

2. Are the words complained of, or any of them, with the special meanings ascribed to them in questions later, defamatory of the plaintiff?

3. Do the words complained of in the first paragraph of the said article mean (or would be understood to mean):
   (a) that the plaintiff is a person of intemperate habits?
   (b) that the plaintiff is a sponger?
   (c) that the plaintiff is unjustifiably abusive in his dealings with others?
   (d) that the plaintiff possesses only an inadequate acquaintance with the grammar and syntax of the English language?

4. Do the words in the second paragraph of the article mean (or would be understood to mean):
   (a) that the plaintiff in his private capacity displays vanity, shallowness or cunning?
   (b) that the plaintiff in his private capacity is not to be taken seriously?

5. Do the words in the third and fourth paragraphs mean (or would be understood to mean):
   (a) that the plaintiff is a snob?
   (b) that the plaintiff is ashamed of his origin?

6. Do the words in the eighth and ninth paragraphs of the article mean (or would be understood to mean) that the plaintiff started *Kavanagh's Weekly* out of malice or hatred

towards certain periodicals, newspapers, publishing or literary agencies, therein specified or Radio Éireann, because of their refusal or neglect to employ him.

7. (a) Are the words complained of statements of fact or expressions of opinion, or partly one and partly the other?

(b) Insofar as you find that they are statements of fact, are such statements of fact true?

(c) Insofar as you find that they are expressions of opinion, do such expressions of opinion, or any of them exceed the limit of fair comment?

8. Assess damages.

When the questions had been settled, Thomas Connolly, counsel for Kavanagh, attempted to get Teevan to rule out 'fair comment' as one of the grounds of defence. Teevan, while unsure, eventually refused to do so: 'I rule with very considerable hesitation and doubt. My preference is that it is not a case in which fair comment arises at all in the defence because, in my view, were I deciding this matter for myself, the article is a pen picture of the person, Patrick Kavanagh, and is not a criticism of any work of Mr Kavanagh's.' He added that only one work of Mr Kavanagh's was named in the profile – the poem, 'The Great Hunger'. This had been brought in, incidentally, to illustrate another facet of the character of the man who was supposed to be portrayed in the article.

'It is not sufficient or proper,' Teevan ruled, 'to lift out of an author's work, pieces or statements or phrases and put them down as descriptive of his character without in many cases using quotation marks.'

The name of the article, he stated, and what it purported to be, its opening, its constitution, showed that it was clearly an article descriptive of Mr Kavanagh himself, his personality and character, and in his view, fair comment did not arise. However, he felt obliged to allow it to remain as an issue because he had doubts whether he could withdraw it from the jury at this stage.

James MacMahon, counsel for the defence, submitted that as no evidence had been called for the defence, they had the right to address the jury last. Connolly, counter-argued, contending that because the defence had produced documents they had not the right to last say.

On the question of the order of closing statements, the judge ruled that Mr MacMahon for *The Leader* should address the jury first, then Mr Connolly on behalf of Kavanagh and then Mr Fitzgerald would conclude on behalf of the printers, Argus Ltd. After the tour de force that was his cross-examination of Kavanagh, the defence team were not using Costello for the summing-up.

The jury then returned to the courtroom and the closing addresses began.

James MacMahon said that there were two defences. The first was that the article taken as a whole was not libellous, and was not, to any fair-minded reader, a defamation of Mr Kavanagh and would not reduce the esteem in which he was held by a reasonable man. If they were satisfied about that it was the end of the case. If they were not satisfied fully as to that, and if they were satisfied that there were portions of the profile which, even reading the article as a whole and taking the good with the bad, carried reflection on him, there was still the defence of 'fair comment'.

What was written about Mr Kavanagh, or at least a portion of it, was a legitimate exercise by *The Leader* and the author of the profile of the right of public criticism, and that what was said was within the bounds of fair comment. It was criticism on a matter which might properly be said to be public criticism of the works of Mr Kavanagh as an author and writer and his own character and personality as relating to his work.

Comment was fair if made by a fair-minded individual, although he might be a man holding prejudiced or obstinate views. If the jury were satisfied that what was complained of in this article were views that a fair-minded man might express, and they were views expressed about Mr Kavanagh or his character in relation to his work, *The Leader* then submitted that the profile, and the parts of it to which exception had been taken, were protected by the defence of fair comment.

'If you are satisfied that what is dealt with in the profile is Mr Kavanagh in his public character – as an author, poet, an authority on literature – and his ideas – whether on literature, economics, on morality, on theology, or on a variety of public matters on which he has written – if you are satisfied that these are the subject matters about which the profile was written, then it is a matter of public interest and a matter on which the right of free speech gives the right of fair comment.'

Ridicule, MacMahon argued, could be a legitimate weapon of criticism, and comment might be fair, even if it took the form of ridicule. It was often the most appropriate and quickest weapon for exposing the falseness of a writer's ideas. Accordingly, it could still be fair comment even if the writer criticised was made to look ridiculous.

The profile should be read as a whole, he asserted. The question for the jury on 'libel or no libel' was what impression was made on the mind of a reasonable reader – what total impression? It was not open to Mr Kavanagh to pick out a bit here and a bit there and to say that the jury must consider it apart from what was in the rest of the profile, because what was said in the rest of the article might entirely remove the sting in the chosen part. If there was a sting in the profile, it was more than removed by what came at the end of the article.

MacMahon argued: 'It has been the practice of newspapers for a very long time to accept articles or contributions from people who do not sign them at all or who sign them with a pseudonym. That might be necessary for a variety of reasons, the contributor might be in some official position where publicity could not attach to his name or a professional man who could not use his name because it would be self-advertisement – there might be a variety of reasons that for perfectly honest motives, he didn't want his name to appear.

'It is perfectly well understood in the newspaper world, and it is a tradition of newspaper practice that the identity of a man, who gives them his work on that understanding, is not disclosed. The practice is so well established that it is now recognised as a rule of law. The absence of the author of the profile's identity was no hardship on the plaintiff and his case. Mr Kavanagh stated that it was a palpable libel and if it was it could be treated at face value and it did not matter who wrote it.'

With regard to the initial correspondence in the case, MacMahon argued that the plaintiff had been offered an apology subject to his indicating what was libellous in the article. All that he needed to do was write one more letter stating what exactly he was complaining about. Was it not clear from what had happened subsequently that he did not want an apology? He wanted money. Mr Kavanagh regretted being offered an apology and side-stepped receiving one because he wanted it to come to court, where he would have to go, if he were going to be awarded money.

His character should have been more valuable to him than any compensation he could get in this action. Yet, having regard to the time necessary for the legal system to work, he allowed the profile to run against him in the intervening months instead of having his character vindicated at once by a formal apology.

The jury were entreated to consider also Mr Kavanagh's conduct as a witness. Did he show himself to be a candid and truthful witness? If he considered the profile a palpable libel on him, had he any motive for evasion or concealment of facts?

MacMahon went on to describe the plaintiff's demeanour in court – that Kavanagh showed himself to be a man who was anxious not that the truth be clearly established and that his character should be vindicated on facts, but that the action should be bolstered up no matter what Mr Kavanagh had to do or say in the witness box to do so.

'Was he animated by spleen against *The Leader* rather than a desire to repair a fancied injury to his character?'

Mr Kavanagh had said that the late D.P. Moran's contribution to national freedom was not significant, that it was a very small part, and that it was only in theory that Mr Moran's son and daughter were behind *The Leader* – that new men had come in and revitalised it in an offensive way.

Mr Kavanagh's attitude had not been straightforward. Was it credible that he had not read the article in *The Bell* by his friend John Ryan, which described the hardships inflicted on a young writer by the government and of police bullying? Did the jury think for one moment that that evidence was true? The plaintiff had been bolstering up his own case with falsehood and now he was pretending to be injured and defamed in his character by a very mild account of something which John Ryan had given a much more colourful version of in *The Bell* in order to display Mr Kavanagh as a hero.

'You will have to make up your minds what kind of article, on the whole, this is,' MacMahon told the jury. 'The controversy here is – is this a serious literary article, about an author, done in a serious way by a person who had made a serious study of Mr Kavanagh's works, and who was interested in commenting on Mr Kavanagh's mind or spirit or intellect as a writer – or was it merely a personal attack on Mr Kavanagh put forward under a cloak?

'Was the motive behind this an attack on the private character of Mr Kavanagh's moral character or any character – except his as an author, a writer, an authority?'

Any consideration of Mr Kavanagh's personal character would be quite a different thing to dealing with his public life.

As to Mr Kavanagh's reaction to the profile: 'Isn't it clearly a bogus and simulated offence?' He had not objected when Mr Hubert Butler had criticised him in similar terms.

'Put in a very crude form, it is roughly the gist of this article, namely that Mr Kavanagh's genius is as a poet ... that he has wasted his time laying down the law on morality and theology and that he should stick to the things for which he has a gift. Was it fair criticism to say that he was a superficial observer of city life? Was Mr Kavanagh's character affected by whether he was regarded as an acute or superficial observer of city life?'

MacMahon continued: 'You have heard extensively quoted Mr Kavanagh's writings, aren't these words "truth, life and reality" of frequent occurrence, and do they not mean anything fixed, but what Mr Kavanagh wants them to mean. He said himself in the box that if he told the truth he would be crucified.'

When MacMahon proceeded to say that Mr Kavanagh had admitted that parts of his poem 'The Great Hunger' were obscene, Mr Justice Teevan interjected to say that Mr Kavanagh did not say that they were obscene in the eyes of the police.

Connolly for the plaintiff said: 'He said that the police officers never mentioned obscenity or the Act.'

After discussion between the counsels as to what Mr Kavanagh's evidence on the subject was, Mr MacMahon stated that in other words Mr Kavanagh had said that the standards of the law in regard to obscenity were not true standards.

'I am afraid he did not say that,' Justice Teevan said.

'I am putting this as an argument to the jury, my Lord,' MacMahon explained. 'I am submitting that this is an inference that can be drawn about the poem "The Great Hunger".'

MacMahon stated: 'Sociological understanding is not Mr Kavanagh's strongpoint, though, why should it be? He has given us his handful of poems, the pard-like spirit of Poetic Truth flashes for all to see through the maddeningly entangled brushwood of contemporary life.'

MacMahon wrapped up his address to the jury: 'The pard-like spirit; an immortal phrase in the English language written by one of the greatest of lyrical poets about another poet. The author of this article concluded by saying that that phrase is truly applicable to Mr Kavanagh. Could greater praise be given to any poet?'

On this note the court was adjourned until the following day.

Chapter 16

'The great asset of the fine brain God had given him'

'A man who had started without any particular assets, except the great asset of the fine brain that God had given him, of which he made such fine use,' Thomas Connolly said of Kavanagh in his closing address.

Connolly asked the jury to consider his client's origins. He had started out from a small tillage farm of some thirty acres in County Monaghan, one of a family of nine. Being a small farmer's son there were 'no assets or the advantages of birth'. He had but the ordinary schooling of a farmer's son. Yet by 1938 he had *The Green Fool* published by a London firm of publishers. In 1939 he decided definitely to embark on a journalistic and literary career and almost immediately he was able to establish himself in Dublin journalism. He was two years with the *Irish Press*, followed by a permanent position from 1944 until 1947 with the *Standard*. In 1947 his poem 'The Great Hunger' was published and in 1948 his novel *Tarry Flynn* appeared and was praised by critics all over the world.

'In this case,' said Mr Connolly, 'it was clear that they were dealing with a very remarkable man quite out of the ordinary in intelligence. Nevertheless he was a product of the Irish free educational system, which as long as it was able to point to men of that stamp amongst its product, had no need to fear any criticism or sneers from anonymous writers.'

He went on to point out that Kavanagh's position in the world of letters was outstanding, not only in Ireland but all over the English-speaking world and that this had been demonstrated during the case. In 1948 his work had been included in two anthologies of English poetry. In 1949 it was well represented in a New York publication *1000 Years of Irish Poetry* and in 1952 it was represented again in *1000 Years of Irish Prose*.

The seal was set on his reputation in *The Faber Book of Twentieth-Century Verse* published by Faber in 1953, including poets from all over the world. He was one of only six Irish writers, going back to the beginning of the century, who were represented in it.

The jury could accept Mr Kavanagh as having reached the peak of eminence in his profession, a man about whose reputation any journal must be careful. If there was an insult to a man of Mr Kavanagh's position and distinction, it was a matter that a Dublin jury would mark when they arrived at the assessment of damages.

Connolly mentioned the *Daily Express*, the *Manchester Guardian*, the *Observer*, *John O'London's*; reputable English publications to which Mr Kavanagh contributed. There was no trouble in placing his articles, the question was could he keep up with the demand for them.

In 1947 he had signed a contract with Macmillan and its terms showed the high regard that these publishers held Mr Kavanagh in. The suggestion that had been made to discredit him in regard to this matter was preposterous. They had only to look at the contract to see there had been no breach of it. At present he was also under contract with the Catholic publishers Hollis and Carter to write a book on Irish shrines. *Kavanagh's Weekly*, during the time it ran, had made its mark in Dublin journalism and Mr Kavanagh had been an important contributor to it.

The profile had dealt, in part, with Mr Kavanagh's circumstances and particularly his position as a journalist and broadcaster in 1952: 'I would suggest that there is an implication in that profile that at the time Patrick Kavanagh was a man without employment who had lost his employment from five different institutions because of the views he was expressing, and that as a journalist and a writer generally he was on the shelf.

'What would any of us think if we lifted a paper and saw ourselves portrayed as hunkering down on a bar stool, uttering malevolent insults, speaking ungrammatically, gulping down drinks surrounded by sylph-like redheads and intellectual blondes? Could this have any other meaning than to hold up the person portrayed to contempt and ridicule? If it does, it is libel. That is the short answer to it.'

Connolly went through some passages from the profile in detail: 'Again there is a sneer – Mr Kavanagh is the proprietor of "ultimate truth". He has never said so, or laid claim to that. I will say no more and pass on … He is represented in the profile as the solid peasant – the cunning country boy and as a pard-like spirit. A cunning peasant or a pard-like spirit? There is a world of difference between the two.

'You are dealing with the action brought by a very eminent man,' Connolly told the jury. 'You have seen the interest taken by the public, showing that you are dealing with a most remarkable man. Certainly the defence is taking a very big onus on themselves and a very great risk if they set out to convince you the jury that this action is not a *bona fide* one but from an ulterior motive. But it goes further. They don't put a tooth in it; they ask you to come to the conclusion that Mr Kavanagh is not a candid or truthful witness.

'One of the grounds on which the defence based this contention was that Mr Kavanagh had stated that he had not seen the articles in *The Bell* on October 1951 until five or six weeks ago although he had a poem in it. Was there any reason why Mr Kavanagh's explanation should not be accepted? It was asking a lot of the jury to find that a man of Mr Kavanagh's eminence was going to come to court and perjure himself on that.

'The second matter on which they had been asked to reach this sweeping conclusion was in regard to the evidence about Mr Brendan Behan. Of course, were it not for the use that might be made, the relationship between Mr Kavanagh and Mr Behan would not be of the slightest significance. In evidence Mr Kavanagh had said with great emphasis that Mr Behan was not and had never been his friend.

'When pressed he said it was a lie to suggest that there had been close friendship between them. Mr Kavanagh had said also that he had found out something about Mr Behan, which,' said Mr Connolly, 'had led to the break.'

As to the inscription in the copy of *Tarry Flynn*: 'In the first place, the jury would enquire – where did this book come from? Where else but from Mr Behan who was being put [forward] as being a close friend of Mr Kavanagh. What kind of friend was it who ran around with the book to Mr Kavanagh's opponents and gave it to them?'

On the question of the assessment of damages, Mr Connolly thought he was correct in saying that for many years past no person in the literary world of Mr Kavanagh's stature had been a plaintiff in these courts. The jury, in assessing damages, could not fail to take into consideration the very severe ordeal that Mr Kavanagh had had to undergo. In Connolly's experience of over twenty years in the courts, he had not seen a plaintiff have to sustain a cross-examination so prolonged and severe.

The defendants had not published an apology and had added insult to injury by making a charge in open court, the proceedings of which had received wide publicity in the newspapers, that Mr Kavanagh had come with a false case and given false evidence.

The final statement was made by Mr Fitzgerald, for Argus the printers. He said that the primary consideration for the jury was to appraise the man who had made the complaint. Mr Connolly had been at pains to inform the jury of the law in relation to libel, so far as it affected the printers, and impressed on the jury that they must take it as they found it.

'From the position of law there is no escape,' Fitzgerald

stated. 'The only justification for joining my clients as defendants in this case, is that if there is a verdict of libel, my clients are brought in by Mr Kavanagh to take advantage of the legal situation by which – if he can get a verdict – he can grab the money off the printers. He elected to bring us in. You heard his answer that he did not care where the money came from.'

According to Fitzgerald, Kavanagh had set himself up as some sort of universal critic. However, people in glass houses should not throw stones – those who criticise should anticipate that other people would throw stones as well. Fitzgerald referred to certain articles in *The Bell* where 'the very allegations he now complains of, first appeared, and he had done nothing about it. But he waits until much similar material is printed by *The Leader*, then he complains. That, of course, destroys his case, unless he has some escape from that position. Kavanagh is no fool. He is a distinguished poet, literary writer, and a man apparently with a fine command of the English language, and in that witness-box he was eminently fit to understand questions put to him and to give clear answers at once.'

It was for the jury to decide if he had done so.

'If you have measured Mr Kavanagh up,' Fitzgerald told the jury, 'I think you will find the article, taken as a whole, gives a more than accurate profile of him.'

It was now time for the judge's charge to the jury. Such was the tension in the courtroom that Kavanagh left as soon as Mr Justice Teevan began his address. Peter was worried about where he had gone. It was only during a short recess at 4 p.m.

that he discovered that he had gone to the nearby Four Courts Hotel.

Teevan started off by telling the jury that the 'judgment of this court in this action will depend on your verdict. Nobody else can give any verdict in this case or any judgment one way or the other without your verdict.

'Mr Kavanagh's feelings were undoubtedly seriously hurt and wounded by this article. That may be reasonable or unreasonable, but it doesn't give help to you. It isn't his view of the words, it isn't because he is wounded in his own estimation that matters, but has his character or reputation been wounded in the minds of other people?'

The judge went on to explain that if the jury were of the view that in the eyes and mind of the ordinary man – apart from a particular section of the community, for instance, writers – the profile did defame the plaintiff, they should answer 'yes' to the first question, whether the article as a whole in its ordinary meaning was defamatory to the plaintiff. If, on the other hand, they found that no reasonable man would come to a conclusion that it was contrary to the plaintiff's status, then they should answer 'no' to the question.

'Any printed or written words which tend to lower a person in the estimation of right-thinking men, or tend to expose him to hatred, or to contempt, or to ridicule, or a false statement about a man to his discredit, is a libel. It must be an assumption that can be reasonably formed by the community as a whole – at least those who would read this printed matter – and not any section of the community.'

He emphasised that no matter how cruel or bitter the

words were, no matter how keen the switch with which Mr Kavanagh had been beaten by the words published about him, unless they lowered him in the minds of reasonable people reading the article, there was no defamation.

The jury would have to consider when they read the article through, whether they were getting a pen sketch of Patrick Kavanagh, the man himself, or a rapid survey of his literary works as a critic and as a poet. Although there was very considerable and almost unrestricted scope for criticism in this country – and rightly so – it must be criticism of the public person's work or his public life. Once it invaded the private life of the author or politician, it ceased to be entitled to the defence of fair comment. He suggested to the jury that they would find part of the article comment and part fact but taking it all-in-all, did they find it to be a picture of the man's works?

Justice Teevan commented that Mr Costello had taken a rather ingenious way of proving that the article was fair comment and that the facts were true. He had gone through in a vigorous and certainly thorough fashion, over three days, certain of the works of Mr Kavanagh. It was the judge's opinion that Mr Costello did show that a large part of the article was strung together – a sort of daisy chain of quotations and sayings from Mr Kavanagh's own works.

The defence said that this article, taken as a whole, was a sharp, short outline of the central theme or point of view of Mr Kavanagh's in all his works and that the purpose of the article was to show, firstly, that he was our outstanding poet and secondly – what the writer of the profile perhaps did not agree with – his approach to work and to young artists. In other words, the writer gave the reason for the conflict in Mr Kavanagh's mind between the urban and rural environment and showed that his approach to critics coloured his criticism.

The judge itemised certain issues that the jury would have to consider before coming to a verdict. They should take out the salient facts and see if they referred to Kavanagh the man or his criticism, and they should then go on to decide whether they were true or not. They would have to come to the conclusion that if the introductory paragraph of the article and what were presented as scenes of Mr Kavanagh's life could be set apart as facts relating to his private life, then fair comment would not cover that part of the case.

The jury would notice that Mr Kavanagh had no objection to the company of women and actually approved of it, and had no objection to going into a public house. Nor did he object to women going into public houses. But it was the build-up in the context in the article that he objected to.

The jury would also have to ask themselves whether they could isolate the two scenes in the article and what perhaps was another scene – and the reference to the seizure of copies of the book by officers of the state. If they said that these could be isolated and that they were, in fact, defamatory, they would have to put them back into the context and see whether the harm was taken out of them.

The jury were not to be concerned with whether there was anything of exaltation in Kavanagh's criticism or whether it was an egotistical point-of-view. Even if the purpose of the article was to show Mr Kavanagh was the best, or the worst, living poet, if it was based on facts it would be fair criticism. Mr Kavanagh had been very closely cross-examined about his own criticism and the jury would have to bear in mind whether if, in his articles, he was attacking individuals apart from their literary works: 'If you find this, I think it is only fair that he should be subjected to some criticism. While he admits that his own criticism was corrosive and hard, he said throughout his evidence that what he was attacking was not a man or men, but a point of view.'

As regards the poem 'The Great Hunger' the evidence was that it had been on sale freely since 1942 and there had been no confiscation of it.

The judge felt that the Brendan Behan incident was of little consequence. However, it was clear that, not only in this instance but in other instances also, Mr Kavanagh lacked candour in answering things properly, in getting done with them and passing on to something else. If they found the facts as put to them by the defence about Mr Kavanagh's reliability as a witness to be true then this would lessen their concern for him in regard to the estimation of damages.

Referring to an article in which it had been said that Mr Kavanagh was criticising Rome, the judge said that this had nothing whatever to do with the issue. As regards references to the 'Ardagh Chalice' and 'Father John' and the 'Catholic Cultural League', Mr Kavanagh was being criticised strongly, but if he wrote about a thousand priests it did not affect the truth, or otherwise, of the article or whether it was defamatory or otherwise.

The judge said that he would accept a majority of nine on the questions.

At the conclusion of the judge's address the jury foreman asked if they were to take it that if they answered 'No' to the first question, they were to stop there? And if they answered 'Yes' were they to proceed to the other questions?

Justice Teevan said that although he had ruled otherwise the previous day, he was now inclined to think that Mr Fitzgerald had been right and that if the answer to the first question was 'No' the other questions should not be answered. It was a question of 'libel or no libel'.

The jury retired at 5.10 p.m. to consider their verdict. Once they had filed out, Sir John Esmonde, counsel for the plaintiff, addressed the judge: 'Your Lordship just said that if the jury answer question number one that there was no libel, then the "innuendos" go out.'

'Not necessarily,' Teevan replied.

'I am afraid that is the question your lordship created.'

MacMahon for *The Leader* then asked the judge to direct the jury that the 'innuendoes' were taken away. His lordship replied that he had practically done so. Fitzgerald, for Argus Ltd, not surprisingly supported MacMahon's application.

Following intense discussion in the absence of the jury the judge recalled them at 5.54 p.m. and gave them further directions. He instructed them that if they answered yes to the first question then they were to answer all of them, but if they answered no, then they should stop at that point.

That having been clarified for them, the jury retired again at 6.14 p.m.

'LET'S GET MISERABLE AGAIN'

The jury returned at 6.45 p.m. In total they had been considering their verdict for a little over seventy minutes. Given the length of the trial and the drama and tension of the evidence it seems a short spell. Perhaps they were anxious to get home for the weekend. Peter Kavanagh had been dubious about the make-up of the jury from the beginning of the trial. They 'were drawn from the upper-lower class of Dublin shopkeepers and one look at them was enough to convince even the most optimistic of us that only a miracle could save us.' The foreman handed the sheet to the court clerk, answering 'no' to the questions put to him. Fitzgerald asked for judgment with costs in favour of the defendants. The judge granted a stay of execution with regard to costs in case there was an appeal.

It did not seem that the jury had much trouble coming to their verdict. The judge excused the members from further service for five years. Peter rushed out of court to the hotel where Patrick was waiting: 'No, no, no, to every question,' he announced.[1] According to Peter, Patrick later expressed anger with him for not sugaring the pill, although, it is not clear how the bad news could have been delivered in any other way.

There had been seven senior counsel and three junior counsel engaged. 256 questions had been put to Kavanagh by his own counsel, 1,267 in cross-examination by Costello and another 71 by counsel for Argus, the printers. A re-examination took up a further 87 questions. It had been a nightmare for Patrick. The trial had been about him, not about *The Leader* article.

Many people thought that he had, in fact, been the defendant. It was an easy mistake to make.

Kavanagh felt that the trial had turned into a popularity contest about him, rather than a simple libel case, if ever a libel case could be simple. He had endured the ordeal of cross-examination, suffered what he saw as public mortification and then found himself rejected by a jury of his peers.

Peter Kavanagh observed at close-hand the effect the trial had been having on his brother: 'His throat began to bother him. He could barely swallow food.' According to Peter, Patrick's supporters had begun to desert him as the trial went on: 'His friends, sensing defeat, began to hedge.'[2]

According to the *Irish Press* Patrick 'did not conceal his disappointment at the verdict'. But he had some fight left. He told their reporter: 'In view of the possibility of an appeal to the Supreme Court I am not at liberty to make a statement.'[3]

It was said at the time that the real winner of the case, in fact the only winner, was McDaid's pub, because it had been given so much free publicity. As Paddy O'Brien, celebrated barman at McDaid's, put it: 'Though the case ruined Patrick's health, everyone in the country was talking about him and as many came here [to McDaid's] to see the place that had been in all the papers ... McDaid's became a national institution.'[4]

After the jury found against him Patrick was distressed, but not for long according to his brother. His natural resilience quickly asserted itself. By that evening he had recovered his poise. Peter recalled: 'After an interval of silence we both returned to normal. The comedy of the decision in the law case grew in wonderment as we talked. We began to smile, then to laugh, and finally we both fell into uncontrollable paroxysms of laughter. We roared until we were almost ill, and the more we tried to sober up the wilder the laughter became.'[5]

'We lost not a thing,' Patrick said, 'while the opposition will be bankrupt, even disgraced for doing down Ireland's only poet.'

'Our counsel also lost,' Peter pointed out.

'Lost,' said Patrick, 'all they lost was their reputation … Let's get miserable again or we may lose our sympathy.'[6]

Now that the case was lost Peter felt that 'in retrospect it is clear Patrick would have been better had he taken his own advice, swing freely, be totally himself.'[7] He believed that his brother had tried to appear too respectable and middle-class in front of the jury.

Anthony Cronin was of the opinion that Kavanagh had, subconsciously or otherwise, been seeking a form of literary martyrdom, while Costello had merely gone about his business of trying to win the case for his client. It had worked out for both of them: 'As a means of raising money the trial was certainly a flop, since the jury found there was no libel at all. However, as an exercise in martyrdom, it was, up to a point anyway, a superb success.'[8]

It also had another unintended consequence, Patrick became even more notorious.

'He took some consolation from what nowadays would be called the coverage it got … Costello, whatever else he had done, had certainly succeeded by his cross-examination and the responses it elicited in adding to the Kavanagh legend. People who had never read a line of poetry, who were not sufficiently in the Dublin swim to have heard the Kavanagh jokes and the Kavanagh stories, who did not frequent his pubs, were now aware that they had a poet in their midst. "I'm as famous as de Valera," he said one day.[9]

As his great adversary Behan had put it, perhaps not entirely seriously, there is no such thing as bad publicity except your own obituary.

Chapter 17

'Those wigged folk from their lofty positions of importance'

John Ryan declared that Patrick 'was familiar enough with litigation to realise that the costs were going to be enormous; and they were.'[1] So many parties were involved in the action, 'printer, publisher … solicitors holding watching briefs, senior counsels, junior counsels, bewigged snoopers from other courts, that the whole scene resembled nothing so much as a flight of scald-crows descending on a potato field.'[2]

There was quite a lot of sympathy for Patrick. He received a number of letters. Christina McDonald of Hatch Street wrote:

> There is many a man and woman amongst us who would like to tell the truth but we haven't got the guts. I didn't go to the court because I couldn't watch a soul being heckled by those wigged folk from their lofty positions of importance. You may have lost the case but you have not lost because there must be some that still believe in truth – from the red-haired wench who used to share your table at lunch in the Country Shop.[3]

Tom Dunne, editor of *The Irish Countryman*, official organ of the Irish Creamery Milk Suppliers' Association, wrote from Limerick:

> … just a line from an old and lasting friend. Your stand was quite magnificent and evinced the most tremendous interest among the few people in provincial Ireland who do not belong to the 'dumb, disciplined, regimented majority'. Everywhere I go there is a fine expression of fearless opinion among educated people, with independent minds, that your action was the type of action that proves, beyond all doubt, that trial-by-jury has great and grave limitations.
>
> … The trouble was, of course, that a jury that might as well have been empanelled to hear a cattle-stealing case, did not quite comprehend all that was involved, and your stature in Irish letters. Indeed their decision illustrates, pretty accurately, the level of thinking in this country. One thing that is being said, on all sides, is that, while the O'Caseys and the Shaws bombarded from without, you stood your ground and told the truth with your feet planted firmly on the soil of Ireland. It was a mighty achievement and one for which recognition and admiration, in full measure, will come some day.[4]

Even Kavanagh's old adversary, Hubert Butler wrote to commiserate:

> I am afraid you have had a terrible ordeal and I am so sorry. Like everybody else I have been following the case with interest and have marvelled at the fine spontaneous things you said under circumstances that must have imposed a terrible strain on you.
>
> I am grateful for the generous way in which you referred to my 'Bell' article, but you were quite right in thinking it was written

without any personal spleen. I had tracked down all your writings which I could find and read them with the keenest interest even when they seemed an assault on my sacred shibboleths, for you never write anything that is dull or flat.

Is it possible for a writer to live in Ireland? Often to me it seems a hopeless attempt, but then I am a very much more unproductive and inarticulate person than you are and therefore hardly a test case ... I hope though, you don't get discouraged altogether about Ireland. You are badly needed over here, a brave voice, always saying what you think and not troubling, like everybody else, about whether it is 'discreet' or popular.[5]

The case had caused some ripples abroad. The *Spectator* ran an article called 'The Kavanagh Case' on 9 March written by Jack White, formerly London editor and then literary editor of *The Irish Times*:

Nothing sells the papers in England, they tell me, like a nice, juicy murder ... But even an Irish editor has his day ... nothing, it is now evident sells the papers in this country like a nice, juicy libel action ... the writs for libel fall as plentifully as leaves in October ... The actions do not often come to court as the newspaper proprietors have discovered that it is generally cheaper to settle. The last few weeks may give them cause to revise their economics. The action of Patrick Kavanagh against *The Leader* magazine sold so many thousand extra copies of the papers that one begins to wonder whether it would not pay the proprietors to bring down libel actions on their own heads, in the interest of circulation.

The catch, of course, is that few actions can boast a plaintiff as colourful as Mr Kavanagh.

The Leader is a little fortnightly magazine which fills for

Ireland the place occupied by the weekly reviews such as the *Spectator* in Britain. After a long history of courageous but conservative nationalism, it has been rejuvenated in the last couple of years by the co-option of a number of brilliant young men, chiefly from University College Dublin, and its articles on political and economic subjects are now some of the best published in Ireland. Part of its brightening-up campaign has been a series of profiles of which the article on Patrick Kavanagh was one.

... For two full days in court and parts of two other days he [Costello] hammered away. The crowd in court and the newspapers lapped it up. From first to last *The Irish Times* gave the hearing forty-three columns, or round about twenty-nine yards of print.

Those who knew Costello's devastating form were prepared to see him knock the peasant-poet out of the ring. Both poets and peasants are notoriously wily in argument. Kavanagh was determined not to let anybody get him in a corner. He ducked, side-stepped, swerved, and in the intervals swung some haymakers, which to judge by the response from the ring-side, seemed to be registering with a clang. As the event proved, it was Costello who was registering on the score-card.[6]

And yet, despite the pummelling he had received, there was still some fight left in Kavanagh and some hope too. Almost immediately the notion of an appeal was floated. Kavanagh's solicitors were strongly of the opinion that there were solid grounds for an appeal to the Supreme Court on points of law.

A Kavanagh Appeal Fund Committee was set up at a meeting in the Gresham Hotel in early March. Its members were Joseph Hone, John Ryan, Eoin 'the Pope' O'Mahony, Eamon Ginnell and Elinor O'Brien. The committee cast their net far and wide in their search for contributions as the following letter illustrates:

Dear Miss O'Brien,
I have just received the registered letter signed by yourself and two other members of your committee, enclosing the form of application for the Patrick Kavanagh Fund and a number of letters from persons to whom application have been made. Also stubs of a receipt book. I am retaining the duplicated appeal form but returning all the other matter instantly. I have no need to see such letters and cannot understand why you have sent them to me. The question of whether anyone has contributed to this defence fund is of minor importance from my point of view, what I want to know is whether it is something to which I ought to make a contribution myself, and in order to know that, I should want to know what this libel suit is about, who is libelled, what the libel is, and what injustice Mr Kavanagh may have suffered. On the whole case, I am entirely in the dark.
Yours
T.S. Eliot.[7]

Evidently, Eliot had his worries dispelled to judge from the tone of his next letter: 'I have received and read the file of *The Irish Times* which you kindly sent me. The report of the case is of most absorbing interest. I need make no further comment at the moment beyond sending herewith a contribution to the Patrick Kavanagh Fund …T.S. Eliot.'[8] Eliot gave twenty guineas for the appeal.

John Betjeman was characteristically breezier in the note that accompanied his donation of £10: 'I hope the old boy wins. He deserves to.'[9]

Among the other donors to the Appeal Fund were Jack B. Yeats and Anew McMaster. It was not just artistic types that supported the Appeal Fund; one of Patrick's bookies, J.J. Fogarty, also gave a donation.[10] However, not everybody approached was willing to contribute. Hubert Butler, despite the supportive letter he sent to Patrick immediately after the outcome of the case, was one of those:

> I suppose the basic reason for not responding is that I have a huge overdraft and can only pay it off by many pettifogging economies ... But I don't really like libel actions ... I once nearly started one myself ... But I don't think the ruining of *The Leader* if he wins, or disappointment and disaster for himself if he loses the appeal, will help the cause of writers generally. Only the Philistines will rejoice, who love to see writers at each other's throats, and of course, the lawyers.[11]

Basil O'Connell, as a legal man himself had strong views on the prospect of an appeal:

> Though naturally I sympathise with anyone who gets into sadness and worry, I cannot support Mr Kavanagh. Those who live by the pen and who have to dip their pen in acid to titillate the jaded palate of the public, must be prepared for the inevitable comeback when they have acid sprayed on them.
>
> As a prosecuting officer of long experience I know so well that it can never work out right to submit oneself to cross-examination of one's own character, however much one may try

to lead a decent life. I will guarantee to reduce most any man to tears in the box on the subject of his own character.

I consider therefore that Mr Kavanagh was ill advised ever to submit to cross-examination, even to take a case to rehabilitate himself. I consider that opposing counsel was (with an eye to the jury) gentler on him than he might have been. I consider therefore that Mr Kavanagh is throwing good money away in pursuing the matter further.[12]

Dr Joseph Walsh, the Archbishop of Tuam, was more circumspect: 'I really know nothing about the facts. Indeed I am anxious to help Mr Kavanagh but I think it is better not to move for the present.'[13]

Daniel Duffy a priest in Inniskeen, Kavanagh's home parish in Monaghan, was more forthcoming:

I am prepared to contribute the modest sum of £2 to help defray Mr Kavanagh's expenses, that is, if such a sum is acceptable. When the *Weekly* was in danger of collapse, I made a similar offer and it was returned. May I say that I do not regard an 'independent mind in Irish life' as being at stake. I do this for Kavanagh as a friend and a critical admirer. I am sorry he brought this libel case at all.

The now famous profile did not lower him in my estimation when I read it at the time. It was a literary caricature, amusing and pungent but like all caricature, playfully distorted. Only the extremely literal could cant at it.[14]

On 18 February, Flann O'Brien writing as Myles na gCopaleen in an article in *The Irish Times* entitled 'Wigs on the Green' complained of the overcrowding in the court and the poor acoustics. He had attended but he had been forced to read the papers to find out what had been said.[15]

Less than one month after the case had concluded, notice of appeal was lodged in the Supreme Court. Among the grounds of appeal listed were:

1. That the finding of the jury that the article complained of was not in its ordinary meaning defamatory of Mr Kavanagh, was such as no reasonable jury could or ought to have made.
2. That the jury could not have apprehended the real issues to be tried and were influenced by considerations not legally applicable in making their finding on that first question.
3. That the finding of the jury was against the weight of evidence and that it was perverse.
4. That the trial judge misdirected the jury in giving certain directions to them, and that he misdirected himself in law, in allowing, notwithstanding direction, cross-examination of Mr Kavanagh to prove the alleged truth of libellous statements of fact contained in the article complained of, and in allowing the truth of such statements to be an issue at the trial when justification had not been claimed as a defence.
5. That the judge misdirected himself in law in ruling that counsel for Argus should address the jury after counsel for Mr Kavanagh.
6. That the judge misdirected himself in law by ruling that evidence of witnesses to be tendered on behalf of Mr Kavanagh was ruled inadmissible.
7. That the trial itself was unsatisfactory.[16]

Peter Kavanagh reported that one of the jury had written to Patrick on hearing that the libel verdict was to be appealed.

One of the grounds given for the appeal was that the jury had acted unreasonably in coming to their verdict. This particular jury member took it as an affront and demanded an apology from Patrick.[17]

Patrick's combative nature quickly re-asserted itself. In May 1954 he wrote to Peter in London: 'The appeal of mine is definitely on ... they were almost sure, up to the end, that I'd never be able to bring an appeal. I have been sowing a few lies about who subscribed – Ezra Pound and Somerset Maugham ...'[18]

In June, Kavanagh's solicitor, Rory O'Connor, asked for £600 on account to cover his costs: 'As you know the verdict came as a very great surprise to everybody and our counsel takes the view that the trial of the action was unsatisfactory. We consider that it would be unreasonable to ask us and our counsel to proceed further with the action unless we receive a substantial sum on account of our costs and we calculate that a sum of £600 would be a reasonable sum to enable us to continue with the action.'[19]

He was of the opinion that, having studied the transcripts, they had an excellent chance of overturning the verdict. Despite the work of the Appeal Committee, Kavanagh had nothing like £600 to his name. He told O'Connor that such a demand would have the effect of scuppering the appeal.

In July the solicitors tried one more time: 'I must implore upon you again that I am not prepared to undertake any work on the case until I have some money on hand with which to pay some money to counsel on account of fees due to them and to have some cash on hand for myself to cover the work which I have already done in the case.'[20]

Kavanagh was having nothing of this pressure. He called their bluff, if bluff it was. He wrote back: 'Relative to your last letter to me … I cannot help coming to the conclusion that you, if you ever glance at the newspapers, must know about the economics of creative writing. I would consider it an insult to you to suggest that you did not know or that you equated every spiritual and mental activity with money. You must therefore be well aware that I could not within any foreseeable future produce £600 and your letter is tantamount to saying that you are not going on with the appeal.

'Let me know definitely so that I can make a public statement on the subject and clear the air.'[21]

As one anonymous contributor of £1 to the Appeal Fund put it:

> One may agree with the verdict
> One may applaud the counsel
> But one may also honour the poet
> It will take a lot of these to defray those costs[22]

O'Connor went ahead with the case without the payment.

Chapter 18

'W.B. Yeats introducing George Moore to the King of the Fairies'

The Supreme Court hearing opened on 16 November 1954. Peter Kavanagh took time off from his work to attend. According to him: 'There was not the same excitement on this occasion as there had been when the case first went to trial. The galleries were occupied but not packed and there was no queue outside hoping for a seat.'[1]

The appeal was heard before the five members of the Supreme Court, the Chief Justice Conor Maguire, Martin Maguire, Cecil Lavery, Kingsmill Moore and Cearbhall Ó Dálaigh.

The typed transcript of the original trial ran to 325 foolscap pages and was read into the record. Sir John Esmonde again represented Kavanagh. He said that Mr Costello in his cross-examination had tried to throw a smoke-screen over the entire case. He argued that their appeal was not based on one point alone but on the accumulative effect of many smaller points.

Mr Justice Kingsmill Moore asked if there had been 'no evidence at all on behalf of the defendants?'

'No evidence on behalf of either defendant,' Sir John commented, 'and it would seem that having regard to the cross-examination of the plaintiff himself, it was reasonable for anyone conducting the case on his behalf to anticipate that there would be some evidence of some kind for them. But there was not.'

It was slow going: by day two of the appeal they had only reached page 185 of the trial transcript. *The Irish Times* reported Esmonde as saying (regarding Costello's introduction of the 'Diplomatic Whiskey' article from the first issue of *Kavanagh's Weekly* into evidence despite the fact that it was not written by Patrick Kavanagh): 'It was a most damnable piece of writing to put before the jury. It was not relevant; it had nothing whatever to do with the issues in the case and must have inflamed the jury beyond all measure.'[2]

The next day *The Irish Times* corrected themselves. Sir John had in fact said: 'It was a most damaging piece of writing.'[3]

Sir John drew attention to the fact that the judge had said the allegation that Mr Kavanagh's poem 'The Great Hunger' had been banned was entirely untrue. Not only was 'The Great Hunger' not banned in Ireland, but the manuscript had been purchased by the state and now reposed in the National Library.

Sir John submitted that the profile was capable of no other interpretation than libel. This was founded, not only on good sense but on good law and on justice.

Peter Kavanagh, who attended each day on Patrick's behalf,

believed that some of the justices were vying with each other to show which of them had the greatest knowledge of English literature.

'Would it be a libel on De Quincey to state he was a drug addict?'[4]

Kingsmill Moore asked: 'Would it not be legitimate to discuss the drinking habits of Ben Jonson in the Mermaid Tavern?'

'No,' answered Connolly, 'such a party was entirely private. Jonson himself made that quite clear when he wrote "On inviting a friend to Supper".' Connolly then recited the lines impromptu:

> And we will have no Polly or parrot by
> Nor shall our cups make any guilty men,
> But our party we shall be,
> As when we innocently met.

The assembled justices were impressed.

Chief Justice Maguire asked: 'Could not George Moore or W.B. Yeats have taken a libel action arising out of the cartoon of W.B. Yeats introducing George Moore to the King of the Fairies?'

'I think that was a harmless cartoon,' Connolly replied.

After seven days of the hearing on 26 November 1954, the court reserved its judgment.

In the meantime, Kavanagh had been as vigilant as ever with regard to his reputation. He wrote to the editor of the *Sunday Empire News* in London: 'I have information that Mr

H.L. Morrow, a contributor to the Irish editions of your paper under the name of I believe McSweeney, has expressed malice towards me. This is to advise you in advance as I wish you no trouble. I have informed my solicitors of the possibility of such a veiled attack, and of my letter to you. I am a journalist and anxious to play the game fairly with newspaper editors … For your information this libellous attack may be contained in an article about a man named Behan, and I strongly advise you to cut my name out of all copy, or any reference to a libel case appeal to the Irish Supreme Court which is subjudice.'[5]

'I AM BAD NEWS'

In a curious postscript to the trial, Kavanagh struck up a relationship with John A. Costello who by the time the case had gone to appeal had become Taoiseach again. The 18 May 1954 was general election day in Ireland. Costello represented Dublin South-East constituency, which covered the Pembroke Road area, and Kavanagh was one of his constituents.

According to Peter Kavanagh, Patrick encountered Costello at the Polling Station. He was coming out of a polling booth when he ran into the politician. Costello shook Patrick's hand and said: 'I hope you have no grudge against me.'

'On the contrary,' Patrick replied, 'I have just voted for you.'

And so began a series of quiet communications between them.[6]

Peter Kavanagh believed Costello felt guilty over having put Patrick through such an ordeal in the witness box and his brother was quick to exploit this guilt. Patrick, as ever alert to the possibilities, sought help in finding a job of some sort. He always liked the idea of having an influential friend in high places. Costello was anxious to help but was wary of any negative publicity if word got out. Kavanagh struck up a correspondence with the politician.

The letters grew progressively more demanding in tone as the months passed by with no result. Costello tried to calm Kavanagh and in a letter dated 16 December 1954 he wrote: 'You may be assured that, though you have not heard from me, I have not forgotten you. I warned you that it would probably take time and not to be too restive. I have been inquiring and will continue my searches.'[7]

Patrick was not to be pacified by mere words. If anything he became even more frantic. On 16 February 1955 he wrote: 'As my economic position has reached the impossible and will force me to get out in the near future, I thought I had better write again to the man who, of all people in Ireland, probably knows me most intimately.

'I appreciate how difficult it is for you to think up things as well as grant them. I suggest two things – which in fact you suggested yourself though I failed to take up the cue at the time. How about getting me a grant from the Arts Council? Would you suggest that I apply? Also, on the News Staff of Radio Éireann, I've had long experience as a journalist ... or anything in the publicity line for Aer Lingus ...'[8]

Patrick had applied for the position of curator of the Dublin Municipal Gallery of Modern Art but had not been successful.[9] This hardly lightened his mood. Similar to the letters he had written to his other powerful patron, Archbishop McQuaid, he hinted to Costello at the possibility of emigration.

Costello was quick to respond. He wrote the very next day: 'I have not forgotten you. Last week I had a conversation with the President of UCD and we discussed the possibility of his using your services as a Lecturer on Poetry – giving lectures around the country. I said that if he could arrange that I would see if I could get the Arts Council to contribute something to the expenses involved, I will. And if that can be arranged soon. In the meantime I would be glad if you would regard this as strictly confidential and mention it to no one.'[10]

Michael Tierney, President of University College Dublin, had been, not incidentally, a staunch Fine Gael activist over the years. As Patrick told Peter: 'He [Costello] is afraid of involving his public life in me. I am bad news to many of his colleagues, no doubt so he is going to do something through a third party.'[11]

Things were looking up for Patrick on the financial front, but by March 1955 he had other matters on his mind. By this point he was involved in an even more desperate struggle.

'SICK IN MIND, BODY AND SPIRIT'

Kavanagh had felt unwell for some time. He told his brother: 'After the law-suit I found that the thought of food appalled. My swallowing apparatus wouldn't work ... I was sick in body, mind and spirit ...'[12] It was statements like this that led his brother to believe that the stress of the trial had weakened his brother's resistance. Peter was not the only one to notice this decline. May O'Flaherty, of Parsons Bookshop recalled: 'This was a bad time for Patrick. The court case took a lot out of him. He never complained but he seemed to be much slower and it was obvious that he was not very well.'[13]

Miss O'Flaherty recounted a meeting with him in the shop when he tried to put a brave face on it: 'Patrick sounded more optimistic than before, when he made his first New Year 1955 visit. He had high hopes of winning the libel appeal and of Mr Costello finding some work for him. But there was no mistaking the fact that he was ill. He looked unwell, constantly coughed and we again encouraged him to visit a doctor.'[14]

While he was proceeding with the appeal he was feeling worse and worse. Early in 1955 he asked a doctor, a relative of Elinor O'Brien, to examine him. By this stage as his biographer points out, such was his physical state that 'coughing, hawking, and spitting had become inseparable from his public image'.[15]

Patrick was resigned to his fate, fearing the worst: 'Very likely it is cancer and it will kill me but to tell you the truth … I don't give a shite.'[16] His worst fears were realised. An X-ray showed up a spot on one of his lungs. In a short space of time Patrick was diagnosed with lung cancer.

He had been drinking heavily since the libel trial, neglecting to eat. He had also been under much stress in the lead-up and aftermath of the trial. His body was in a run-down condition. His consumption of cigarettes must also have contributed. He had smoked from an early age. In fact, Peter recalled incidents from their life in Mucker: 'Another irritation which bothered

Mother was his habit of pilfering money to pay for cigarettes …' Peter also reported that Patrick also used to extract money from his sister Celia for those 'cigarettes that eventually were to lead to his destruction.'[17]

Peter returned from London where he was working at the time, to take charge of the situation. The night before Patrick was due to enter the hospital Peter tidied up the flat on Pembroke Road. On cleaning out the bathroom, he found fifty-eight milk bottles that he put outside the door to be picked up.[18]

So serious was the illness and so pessimistic was Patrick of his prospects that he made a will, bringing it to Searson's pub to be witnessed. Patrick signed it there, the witnesses being a policeman and the barman.[19] It was a home-made will, much like one that his father would have drawn up in Inniskeen for his neighbours. No solicitors were involved. Patrick drank like a condemned man, bringing drink back from the pub to his flat.

The Behan affair still rankled, so he also wrote out the definitive version of events, as he saw it:

A great deal of play was made of the 'Behan' episode in the law case. The first time I had a personal meeting with Behan was when he was painting on a building on Grafton Street. One day he came down and asked me if I would get him a job with the Board of Works, as I knew Raymond McGrath, the architect. I got him a job and as a compliment Behan offered to paint the flat for me free, a job in which I had little interest.

I stood him a drink and apparently gave him a copy of *Tarry Flynn*, an act I totally forgot about. But then I had given away every single copy of every book of mine and have not in my possession any copy but the Cuala edition of 'The Great Hunger'.

On the evening of my giving the book to Behan I appear to have mentioned it to Anthony Cronin who was astonished that I should have done so for a man whom, as far as he was known to me – shouting from the building sites – I disliked intensely.

Behan was closely involved with the writer of the profile and for months before the case, acted as a sort of agent provocateur, racing after me, leering at me, till in the end the opposition knew that they had only to mention his name to get me angry. There appears to be in me a kind of reserve of dignity that makes people like Behan raving mad; they try to get through and are repulsed when they come up against that area of impenetrable defence which defends the soul.[20]

On 1 March 1995, Patrick checked into Rialto Hospital where he was prescribed a course of penicillin. Patrick did not respond to the treatment. After an exploratory operation it was decided to remove his left lung. So serious was the cancer that not only was the entire lung removed, so too was one of Kavanagh's ribs. Immediately after the operation he suffered greatly and there were fears that he would not pull through.

Keith Shaw, the surgeon, was given a copy of *Tarry Flynn* by Kavanagh. Obviously, the Behan incident from the libel case had not put him off giving people signed copies of his work: 'To Keith Shaw MD FRCSI: This simple pastoral as a token of remembrance of a curious happiness I knew when in the Rialto Hospital a year ago.' He added afterwards: 'As promised in exchange for a rib, my own rib.'[21]

That rib was retrieved by Patrick as a souvenir and in later years, he kept it on his mantelpiece to remind himself that, desperate as his situation was, he had in a way once more beaten the odds.[22]

Once he was over the immediate crisis post surgery, life in hospital was good for Patrick. Being cared for by a regiment of women was in many ways his idea of nirvana and he could hold court during visiting hours.

'A STATUE WHEN HE'S DEAD'

Deirdre Courtney had been involved with Patrick for a number of years and had finally broken up with him in the middle of 1954. She had married Willie Manifold in November 1954 and had moved to Limerick. Yet she had not forgotten Patrick. In April 1955, she wrote to John A. Costello informing him of Patrick's grave condition:

> Dear Mr Costello,
>
> I thought perhaps you might like to know that Patrick Kavanagh is in Rialto Hospital following a major operation. He is extremely weak and I personally believe his life is still very much in the balance.
>
> I have been a most intimate friend of his for a very long time. I was with him all during the libel hearing last year. In fact, I was the only person in his company when he received the verdict. From that moment on he stopped eating. He has never since eaten a meal, but has been living on cups of tea. I know that it broke his spirit and I am firmly convinced that his present illness is a direct result of all the awful torture and mental agony he suffered then and ever since. A person of his sensitivity is not just one in a million but one in fifty or perhaps one hundred million.

With good care and freedom from worry as to what is to become of him in his weak state in the future, he may yet pull out of it. But if he is to make the effort that will save his life, he will need hope and an assurance that someone will look after him. It is a poor thing with all the crowing we have about our freedom, if we cannot keep body and soul together in our one and only living poet, the three million of us at home and all the other millions scattered abroad.

As you have been so intimately connected with the event which has been the toughest of his life and as you are now in a position to do something in the matter, I feel you have a duty before God to do what you can for him. If it were possible, a visit from you might give a great lift to his morale. However I appreciate that this might not be easy.

The urgent problem is a first class convalescent home where he can recover his strength. The Irish nation surely owes him that much and an easy mind about his economic state afterwards. A statue when he's dead beside James Clarence Mangan's will hardly ease our troubled consciences if we throw him to the vultures while he's alive.

I hope you will forgive me for intruding on your busy life. I shall reward your efforts by earnestly praying that God may enlighten and direct you in your most responsible position.

Sincerely,

Mrs Deirdre Manifold[23]

Whether as a result of this letter or not, John A. Costello did visit Patrick and, on a separate occasion, so did the president of UCD. Michael Tierney was about to become his new employer. Costello and Tierney had been in discussion with a view to helping Kavanagh out. They arranged for Kavanagh to be appointed as a lecturer. It was hoped that this would allay the ailing poet's financial worries; Tierney confirmed that he would put Kavanagh on the pay-roll of UCD as a lecturer at a salary of £400. All that was expected of him was to give a few lectures each year.

Archbishop McQuaid also turned up. He and Kavanagh may not have fallen out in the previous years but certainly their relationship had lapsed. McQuaid told him that if asked, he would have given evidence at the trial. That certainly would have been a sensation.

Peter, somewhat cynically, was of the opinion that many of Patrick's 'friends' did not expect him to live and that in fact, some of them were even planning his funeral. Even after he left hospital they were unsure if he would survive.[24] His vocal cords, already damaged by his years of smoking, were further impaired by the operation. He spoke with a characteristic hoarse whisper. As he put it himself: 'I am in good form though, as you realise, one lung is not the equal of two, and one gets depressed, somewhat frustrated; there is some discomfort always. But I am not by any means complaining.'[25]

Kavanagh felt he was a celebrity and that at long last, he was being appreciated as a poet in his home country. He revelled in being the centre of attention. However, when he recovered some of his strength his obstreperous nature also returned. Once he had recuperated to a manageable level, it was obvious that he would have to continue his convalescence elsewhere.

As it turned out, the summer of 1955 was one of the warmest on record. The heat hung heavily over the city. Patrick recuperated slowly. He spent his time by the Grand Canal, idling along its banks. As he later wrote: 'For many a good-looking year I wrought hard at versing but I would say that, as a poet, I was born in or about 1955, the place of my birth being the banks of the Grand Canal.'[26]

Here, Kavanagh experienced a spiritual awakening and his poetry flourished with a new strength of purpose. As he described it: 'I want to report about the Grand Canal bank last summer. I report on the part of the bank just to the west of Baggot Street Bridge. Most days last summer in the beautiful heat, I lay there on the grass with only my shirt and trousers on. I lay on that grass in an ante-natal roll with a hand under my head. And because that grass and sun and canal were good to me, they were a particular, personal grass, sun and canal. Nobody anywhere else in the world knew that place as I knew it.'[27]

Like many a man who has survived a close brush with death Kavanagh felt a new lease of life. In the years preceding the court case he had written very little, but now he started again and with a fresh note of optimism in his verse. A new phase of poetry followed as Kavanagh rediscovered his poetic vision. A more, relaxed, optimistic tone emerged. He began to appreciate nature and his surroundings again and took from them his inspiration for much of his later poetry.

At Christmas 1955, he wrote a short note to Archbishop McQuaid: 'This is to wish you all happiness and as a token that I have not forgotten your goodness and kindness and charity. I have nearly created a sensation by staying alive.'[28]

'YOU CAN'T TAKE BRITCHES OFF A HIGHLANDER'

In the middle of all this, on 5 March 1955, the Supreme Court issued its verdict on Kavanagh's appeal. Chief Justice Mr Conor Maguire and Mr Justice Martin Maguire were in favour of dismissing the appeal. However, the other three judges, Cecil Lavery, Kingsmill Moore and Cearbhall Ó Dálaigh, ruled in favour of a re-trial. Costs of the Supreme Court Appeal were awarded to Kavanagh. The court also ordered that costs of the original trial would be dependent on the result of the new trial. But after all Patrick had been through, the outcome of the appeal seemed less important.

The Supreme Court on a majority verdict had discharged the judgment of the original trial, due in the main to the uncertainty caused by the judge in his summing up and in particular the confusion over the questions that were to be put to the jury. The majority held that certain questions regarding innuendoes had been left to the jury and the jury had been directed by the judge to answer these in the negative. They held that this might have influenced the jury in their answer to the first question – whether the article was libellous or not. The trial was therefore unsatisfactory.

Kingsmill Moore was also unhappy about the cross-examination of Kavanagh: 'It is however very easy for a jury, unless carefully and explicitly directed … to regard a successful cross-examination as to credit in the same light as if it was a successful attack on the general character of the plaintiff.'[29]

Kingsmill Moore summed up the case against the *The Leader*'s profile: 'Brilliantly written, in places sardonic, in places sympathetic, it dealt with Mr Kavanagh's poetry and journalism, and his views and character as manifested in his output. It contained also a description of Mr Kavanagh presiding in a public bar over a coterie of submissive acolytes and, by contrast, an imaginary picture of Mr Kavanagh's land of heart's desire, a London literary salon.

'Mr Kavanagh's poetry was given unstinted praise – "The Great Hunger" being described as probably the best poem written in Ireland since *The Deserted Village* – but his prose writings were criticised unfavourably and his views and character were certainly not held up to admiration. The impression conveyed by the article to me, and which would, I think, have been conveyed to most people was that Mr Kavanagh was somewhat of a poseur, unsubtle, opinionated and overbearing. For myself I find it difficult to see how anyone could come to a conclusion other than that Mr Kavanagh was held up to ridicule, though perhaps mild ridicule, and to contempt, though perhaps gentle contempt.'

To read his judgment Kingsmill Moore seemed to have been of the opinion that there was a libel but that it was at the milder end of the scale, so any prospective damages should be small.

The Supreme Court ordered a re-trial. On 15 April 1955 the *Irish Independent* reported that the heavy list for the Easter Law Sittings included sixty-six appeal cases, 'probably the most interesting of which is the libel action of Patrick Kavanagh … Mr Kavanagh's action is in the list for hearing, not before April 25 …'[30]

They were prepared to go through the whole process all over again. Eventually the case was fixed to begin on 23 June.

The Leader and Argus had some incentive to settle. They would have been aware that, even if they won the re-trial and costs were awarded against Kavanagh, they would be unlikely to get enough to cover the fees of their own lawyers. *The Leader* would also have had to take into account that they would have to do without the considerable talents of John A. Costello who was otherwise engaged running the country.

They may also have feared that the outcome of the original case and the well-publicised illness of Patrick Kavanagh might have led to a rise in sympathy for him. Jury trials were always unpredictable. There was little perceived benefit to them in continuing. As Patrick had put it himself in a letter to his brother, this time it was 'all the fun without the worry for I don't really care a damn if I happen to lose. The other side loses in any case.'[31]

In May 1955 Patrick told Peter that the case had been settled. By this stage they had not expected much in the way of damages. As Peter put it in the play he wrote based on the court case, *The Dancing Flame*: 'you can't take britches off a Highlander'.

In the months leading up to the re-trial, there seem to have been some delicate negotiations between the interested parties. Patrick summed up the state of play in a letter to his brother: 'Argus are broke. My lawyers wouldn't drop their fees if it were otherwise. Argus cannot pay. Everyone lost costs.'[32]

On the day it was due to start the case was struck out. The details of the settlement were not made public. However, according to Antoinette Quinn, the lawyers for Kavanagh were paid, and since they had taken the case on a no-win, no-fee basis, the likelihood is that Kavanagh did receive some lump sum.[33]

In his letter to Peter, Patrick had not mentioned the other defendant, *The Leader*. Despite its small circulation, the paper was well supported by its advertisers and presumably had some regular income. However, it does appear that *The Leader* was also on a perilous financial footing. Léon Ó Broin, a high-ranking civil servant, wrote to John A. Costello in April 1955 upon receiving a letter from Nuala Moran:

> It will be a tragedy if *The Leader*, which has been such a force for so long, and which in recent years has been practically the only independent vehicle of criticism in this country, should disappear. It will be a particular tragedy for the Moran family who have been so long associated with the paper, who have contributed so much to it and who, I believe, have never received from it but a bare livelihood.
>
> The letter from Miss Moran does not say what is to happen to her brother who acted as manager of the paper, but it is, I feel, a desperate state of affairs that Miss Moran herself should be reduced to looking out for a shorthand-typist post after being editor of the paper for twenty years.
>
> It occurs to me that there is a national problem here involved and you may consider examination at Government level desirable. If nothing can be done to ensure the survival of *The Leader* special action would have to be taken to ensure the re-instatement of Miss Moran in the Civil Service. As you probably know, having retired from the service so long ago, she can only now be taken back if the 'public interest' machinery is invoked, and if that should become necessary, I hope it will be possible to find a place for her more in keeping with her intelligence and experience that which she so modestly has for herself.[34]

Ó Broin, like Nuala Moran was a Legion of Mary activist, hence his interest in the problem.

So, in a strange coincidence, both sides in the libel case ended up petitioning John A. Costello for help. Costello seemed more sanguine than Ó Broin. His reply was calm and non-committal: having been hired by *The Leader* he could not now as Taoiseach be seen to show favouritism to his former employer:

> I imagine the trouble about giving up *The Leader* arises from the Kavanagh litigation. Things may never come to the point of closing down, but, of course, I have no information whatever on that matter.
>
> I imagine that the best course for Miss Moran to adopt would be to apply for re-instatement in the Civil Service.
>
> In the special circumstances it might be possible that she would be re-instated but you would be the better judge of official requirements in that respect than I am. There are recent examples of re-instatement after a lapse of a long number of years.[35]

The issue of who wrote the profile is a curious mystery that has remained down through the years. According to Antoinette Quinn writing in 1991: 'It is now time to reveal that the author was, as has long been surmised, the poet and diplomat Valentin Iremonger, who was assisted in his labours by a fellow civil servant.'[36] However, when she came to write Kavanagh's biography in 2001 she seemed somewhat more circumspect: 'To this day authorship of the profile has remained shrouded in secrecy. There is now general consensus that Valentin Iremonger was involved either as sole, main or assistant author.'[37] Professor T. Desmond Williams may also have had some hand in the article. Both of them were closely associated with *The Leader* at the time.

Iremonger worked in the Department of External Affairs, which had been seriously attacked by Peter Kavanagh (writing as John L. Flanagan) in the first issue of *Kavanagh's Weekly*. He was a career diplomat and over the years served as Irish ambassador to among other countries, Sweden, Finland and Luxembourg. Iremonger had been poetry editor of *Envoy*. He also produced translations from the Irish language, including *Dialann Deoraí* (*An Irish Navvy*) by Dónall Mac Amhlaigh, and *Rotha Mór an tSaoil* (*The Hard Road to Klondyke*) by Mící Mac Gabhann.

While Iremonger had been among the many suspects beforehand it seems that during the trial the brothers came to believe he was the main writer of the profile judging by a hand-written note from Patrick to Peter: 'Iremonger hated me because I shoved him out of *Envoy* and praised Cronin.'[38]

On the final day of the trial, so tense was the atmosphere Peter recalled how John Ryan had come up to him 'in a fit and told me that Patrick was reporting he knew who wrote the profile and that he claimed they were friends of Ryan.'[39] Iremonger was an associate of Ryan. In fact *Remembering How We Stood*, John Ryan's memoir, takes its name from a poem by Iremonger.

It was evident from the article that the author was well acquainted with Kavanagh's writings, his poetry, his literary criticism and his journalism. The author also seemed to be very familiar with Kavanagh's lifestyle at the time. It was perhaps that and the unkind accuracy of much of the personal descriptions in the profile that goaded Patrick into taking the libel action. Much of what was contained in it had been already covered in a similar fashion in Larry Morrow's 'Meet Mr Kavanagh' character study in *The Bell*. Patrick had also not been bothered by Hubert Butler's criticism of him in *The Bell* as he felt he was treated seriously in that article.

The main difference was the tone. While Morrow had seemed quietly amused, the profile laughed with a sneer. Kavanagh felt he was being mocked from a height by his so-called social betters, patronised for his naïve ways and condescended to even when he was being praised.

Years later Peter Kavanagh recalled: 'Iremonger was one of those associated with the writing of the profile. I will never forget the evening, before the profile was published, when he blew up into a rage with me near the top of Grafton Street, when I brushed off his advances. My brother did not fancy any of these people or their society.'[40]

Looking back on the trial in later life Kavanagh remarked: 'I was too funny and at the same time too damned in earnest. But the key to my failure in this instance was after all a poet's failure for indeed the poet is Justice without her sword ... In the end it was no comedy for me, indeed was the cause of almost snuffing out my light. It was a terrible experience and a difficult one to squeeze comedy out of, when blackguardism won the day.'[41]

In an un-posted letter from Patrick to his solicitor Rory O'Connor dated 22 March 1955, while he was in Rialto Hospital, he mentioned a phone call they had had the previous day: '… it strikes me that the costs and the suggested damages are very lop-sided. I am writing this while waiting for the operation in an hour's time. I feel that the equity of it would be more apparent if the counsel's fees were pared a bit to add a bit to my lump. In view of everything I should get £500.'[42] So it is probable that Patrick did make some money from his ordeal, though it can hardly have been worth it given what he had been through. As Kavanagh saw it, it had taken him from October 1952 to May 1955 to get some reparation. He concluded that letter to his solicitor: 'You'll appreciate that my attitude is a fair one but I know you'll do your best, all to be able to say, "Thank God it's over".'[43]

Endnotes

Chapter 1

1   Peter Kavanagh, *Patrick Kavanagh: A Life Chronicle,* p. 66

2   *Ibid.*, p. 99

3   Peter Kavanagh, *Sacred Keeper* (Self Portrait), p. 347

4   Peter Kavanagh, *Beyond Affection,* p. 54

5   Peter Kavanagh, *November Haggard,* p. 2

6   Anthony Cronin, *Dead as Doornails,* p. 67

7   *Ibid.*, p. 68

8   Peter Kavanagh, *Sacred Keeper,* p. 347

9   John Ryan, *Remembering How We Stood,* pp. 22–23

10   John Cooney, *John Charles McQuaid,* p. 459

11   Peter Kavanagh, *Patrick Kavanagh: A Life Chronicle,* p. 419

12   *Ibid.*

13   John Cooney, *John Charles McQuaid,* p. 142

14   Antoinette Quinn, *Patrick Kavanagh: A Biography,* pp. 135–136

15   Peter Kavanagh, *Patrick Kavanagh: A Life Chronicle,* p. 149

16   Peter Kavanagh, *Lapped Furrows,* p. 57

17   Diary, *Envoy,* May 1951

18   John Ryan, *Remembering How We Stood,* pp. 92–93

19   Robert Greacen, *The Sash My Father Wore,* p. 149

20   *Ibid.*, pp. 149–150

21   Anthony Cronin, *Dead as Doornails,* p. 95

22   J.B. Lyons, *Oliver St John Gogarty,* p. 196

23   Michael MacLiammoir quoted in Peter Kavanagh, *Sacred Keeper,* p. 331

24   Benedict Kiely in conversation 'Humours of Donnybrook', RTÉ, first broadcast 10 January 1979

25   Brian Inglis, *West Briton*, p. 50

26   Robert Greacen, *Brief Encounters*, p. 41

27   Peter Kavanagh, *Lapped Furrows*, p. 50

28   Peter Kavanagh, *Beyond Affection*, p. 48

Chapter 2

1   *Irish Press*, 14 September 1942, p. 2

2   *Ibid.*, 21 September 1942, p. 3

3   'The Jungle of Pembroke Road', RTÉ, first broadcast 6 October 1974

4   *Irish Press*, 6 July 1943, p. 3

5   *Ibid.*, 19 October 1942, p. 3

6   *Ibid.*, 15 October 1943, p. 3

7   *Ibid.*, 20 October 1943, p. 3

8   *Ibid.*, 25 January 1943, p. 3

9   *Ibid.*, 16 July 1943, p. 3

10   *Ibid.*, 27 August 1943, p. 3

Chapter 3

1   Patrick Kavanagh, *The Green Fool*, p. 300

2   *Times*, 21 March 1939, p. 5

3   J.B. Lyons, *Oliver St. John Gogarty*, p. 233

4   *Ibid.*, 22 March 1939, p. 4

5   Antoinette Quinn, *Patrick Kavanagh: A biography*, p. 113

6   John Ryan, *Remembering How We Stood*, p. 115

7   'Meet Mr Kavanagh', *The Bell*, Vol. XVI, No. 1, April 1948, p. 10

8   Peter Kavanagh, *Lapped Furrows*, p. 169

9   Honor Tracy, *Mind you, I've said Nothing*, p. 92

10   *Irish Independent*, 30 July 1940, p. 6

Chapter 4

1   Robert Greacen, *Brief Encounters*, p. 43

2   *Ibid.*, p. 43

3   Peter Kavanagh, *Patrick Kavanagh: A Life Chronicle*, p. 60

4   *Ibid.*

5   *Ibid.*, p. 209

6   Peter Kavanagh, *Lapped Furrows,* p. 84

7   Anthony Cronin, *Dead as Doornails,* p. 69

8   Peter Kavanagh, *Patrick Kavanagh: A Life Chronicle,* appendix, pp. 403–404

9   Self-portrait RTÉ, first broadcast 30 October 1962

10 Peter Kavanagh, *Patrick Kavanagh: A Life Chronicle,* p. 41

11 Anthony Cronin, *Dead as Doornails,* p. 79

12 John Ryan, *Remembering How We Stood,* p. 98

13 J.P. Donleavy, *J.P. Donleavy's Ireland in All Her Sins and in Some of Her Graces,* p. 102

14 John Ryan, *Remembering How We Stood,* p. 108

15 J.P. Donleavy, *J.P. Donleavy's Ireland in All Her Sins and in Some of Her Graces,* p. 102

16 *Ibid.,* p. 106

17 Quoted in John McGahern (ed. Veronica O'Mara), 'The Bird Swift', *PS ... of course,* p. 149

18 Peter Kavanagh, *Sacred Keeper,* p. 348

19 *Irish Times* 18 December 1947, quoted in *Patrick Kavanagh: A Life Chronicle,* p. 216

20 *The Bell* January 1948, quoted in *Patrick Kavanagh: A Life Chronicle,* p. 217

21 Ulick O'Connor, *Brendan Behan,* p. 163

22 Anthony Cronin, *Dead as Doornails,* p. 70

23 Ulick O'Connor, *Brendan Behan,* p. 27

24 Anthony Cronin, *Dead as Doornails,* p. 70

25 *Vogue,* May 1956, quoted in Ulick O'Connor, *Brendan Behan,* pp. 163–164

26 Anthony Cronin, *Dead as Doornails,* p. 74

27 John Cooney, *John Charles McQuaid* p. 459

28 'Meet Mr Kavanagh', *The Bell,* Vol. XVI, No. 1, April 1948, p. 10

29 *Ibid.,* pp. 5–6

30 *Ibid.,* p. 6

31 *Ibid.,* p. 8

32 'Meet the Pope', *The Bell,* Vol. XVI, No. 4, p. 17

33 Anthony Cronin, *Dead as Doornails,* p. 69

34 Leland Bardwell, *A Restless Life,* p. 218

Chapter 5

1   Peter Kavanagh, *Patrick Kavanagh: A life Chronicle*, p. 262
2   Patrick Kavanagh quoted by Anthony Cronin in *No Laughing Matter*, p. 90
3   John Ryan, *Remembering How We Stood*, p. 27
4   Brian Inglis, *West Briton*, p. 75
5   Anthony Cronin, *No Laughing Matter*, p. 109
6   John Ryan, *Remembering How We Stood*, p. 28
7   Honor Tracy, *Mind you, I've said Nothing*, p. 74
8   *Ibid.*, p. 76
9   *Ibid.*, pp. 77–78
10   Anthony Cronin, *Dead as Doornails*, p. 9
11   *Ibid.*
12   *Ibid.*, p. 11
13   *Envoy*, Vol. 1, No. 2, p. 84
14   Anthony Cronin, *Dead as Doornails*, p. 81
15   Peter Kavanagh, *November Haggard*, p. 17
16   John Ryan, *Remembering How We Stood*, p. 95
17   *Ibid.*, p. 97
18   Patrick Kavanagh, 'On Punting', *Kavanagh's Weekly*, Vol. 1, No. 4, 3 May 1952, p. 6
19   Peter Kavanagh, *November Haggard*, p. 17

Chapter 6

1   The *Standard*, 22 February 1946, p. 7
2   *Ibid.*
3   *Ibid.*, 28 February 1947, p. 7
4   *Ibid.*, 7 March 1947, p. 7
5   *Ibid.*, 15 March 1946, p. 5
6   *Ibid.*, 14 June 1947, p. 5
7   *Ibid.*, 31 May 1946, p. 5
8   *Ibid.*, 8 March 1946, p. 5
9   *Ibid.*, 22 March 1946, p. 5
10   *Ibid.*, 10 May 1946, p. 5
11   *Ibid.*, 6 June 1947, p. 5
12   *Ibid.*, 15 August 1947, p. 5

13   *Ibid.*, 17 January 1946, p. 7

14   *Ibid.*, 19 July 1947, p. 5

15   *Ibid.*, 24 January 1947, p. 7

16   *Ibid.*, 21 March 1947, p. 3

17   *Ibid.*, 28 March 1947, p. 3

18   *Ibid.*, p. 7

19   *Ibid.*, 25 April 1947, p. 3

20   *Ibid.*, 9 May 1947, p. 3

21   *Ibid.*, 15 March 1946, p. 5

22   *Ibid.*, 22 March 1946, p. 5

23   *Ibid.*, 26 April 1946, p. 5

24   John Ryan, *Remembering How We Stood,* pp. 91–92

25   The *Standard,* 21 March 1947, p. 7

26   *Ibid.* 16 January 1948, p. 5

27   *Ibid.* 23 July 1948, p. 3

28   Peter Kavanagh, *Patrick Kavanagh: A Life Chronicle*, pp. 182–183

29   The *Standard,* 17 June 1949, p. 3

30   Peter Kavanagh, *Patrick Kavanagh: A Life Chronicle*, p. 182–183

31   Self-portrait RTÉ, first broadcast 30 October 1962

Chapter 7

1   Peter Kavanagh, *November Haggard*, p. 18

2   Patrick Kavanagh, 'The Gallivanting Poet', *New Irish Writing*

3   Anthony Cronin, *Dead as Doornails*, p. 69

4   *Envoy*, Vol. 1, No. 2, p. 81

5   Foreword, *Envoy* Vol. 5, No. 20, p. 8

6   Hubert Butler, *Escape from the Anthill*, p. 153

7   *Ibid.*, p. 154

8   *Ibid.*, p. 155

9   *Ibid.*, p. 156

10   Diary, *Envoy,* Vol. 1, No. 1, p. 87

11   Peter Kavanagh, *Lapped Furrows*, p. 97

12   Patrick Kavanagh, *Almost Everything,* Track 1 (CD)

13   Brian Inglis, *West Briton*, p. 212

14   Anthony Cronin, *Dead as Doornails*, p. 80

Chapter 8

1   Peter Kavanagh, *Patrick Kavanagh: A Life Chronicle*, p. 115
2   *Ibid.*, p. 232
3   *Irish Times*, 10 January 1942, quoted in *Patrick Kavanagh: A Life Chronicle*, p. 138
4   *Kavanagh's Weekly* quoted *in Sacred Keeper*, p. 124
5   Antoinette Quinn, *Patrick Kavanagh: A Biography*, p. 78
6   *Ibid.*, p. 302
7   Peter Kavanagh, *Patrick Kavanagh: A Life Chronicle*, p. 419
8   Anthony Cronin, *Dead as Doornails*, p. 80
9   Peter Kavanagh, *Patrick Kavanagh: A Life Chronicle*, p. 175
10 Ben Kiely in conversation Humours of Donnybrook RTÉ, first broadcast 10 January 1979
11 Peter Kavanagh, *Lapped Furrows*, p. 106
12 Peter Kavanagh, *Patrick Kavanagh: A Life Chronicle*, p. 174
13 Antoinette Quinn, *Patrick Kavanagh: A Biography*, p. 225
14 *Ibid.*, p. 225
15 Leland Bardwell, *A Restless Life*, p. 219
16 *Kavanagh's Weekly*, Vol. 1, No. 7, 24 May 1952, p. 5
17 Robert Greacen, *The Sash My Father Wore*, p. 149
18 Anthony Cronin, *Dead as Doornails*, p. 85
19 *Ibid.*, p. 85
20 Brendan Lynch, *Parsons Bookshop*, p. 41
21 The *Standard*, 21 June 1947, p. 5

Chapter 9

1   Peter Kavanagh, *Beyond Affection*, p. 131
2   Introduction, *Kavanagh's Weekly*, collected facsimile edition 1981, p. 1
3   Peter Kavanagh, *Beyond Affection*, p. 131
4   John Ryan, *Remembering How We Stood* ,p. 97
5   Introduction, *Kavanagh's Weekly*, collected facsimile edition 1981, p. 1
6   Peter Kavanagh, *Beyond Affection*, p. 137
7   *Kavanagh's Weekly*, Vol. 1, No. 1, 12 April 1952, p. 1
8   *Ibid.*, p. 3

9   'Victory of Mediocrity', *Kavanagh's Weekly*, Vol. 1, No. 1, 12
     April 1952, p. 1

10   *Kavanagh's Weekly*, Vol. 1, No. 5, 10 May 1952, p. 3

11   *Ibid.*, No. 3, 26 April 1952, p. 5

12   *Ibid.*, No. 8, 31 May 1952, p. 2

13   *Ibid.*, No. 3, 26 April 1952, p. 2

14   *Ibid.*, p. 2

15   *Ibid.*, No. 4, 3 May 1952, p. 2

16   *Ibid.*, p. 5

17   Brendan Lynch, *Parsons Bookshop*, p. 38

18   Peter Kavanagh, *Beyond Affection*, p. 138

19   *Kavanagh's Weekly*, Vol. 1, No. 10, 14 June 1952, p. 2

20   *Ibid.*, No. 5, 10 May 1952, p. 1

21   Peter Kavanagh, *Patrick Kavanagh: A Life Chronicle*, p. 252

22   Myles na gCopaleen, *Kavanagh's Weekly*, Vol. 1, No. 3, April 26
     1952, p. 4

23   *Kavanagh's Weekly*, Vol. 1, No. 6, 17 May 1952, pp. 4–5

24   Peter Kavanagh, *Beyond Affection*, p. 133

25   John Ryan, *Remembering How We Stood*, p. 103

26   *Kavanagh's Weekly*, Vol. 1, No. 9, 7 June 1952, p. 6

27   *Ibid.*, Vol. 1, No. 13, 5 July 1952, p. 1

28   *Ibid.*, p. 4

29   *Ibid.*

30   Kavanagh Collection, UCD Kav/B/83 (30)

31   John Ryan, *Remembering How We Stood*, p. 103

32   Patrick Kavanagh, *Almost Everything*, Track 1

Chapter 10

1   D.P. Moran quoted in Patrick Maume, *Introduction to the
     Philosophy of Irish Ireland*, appendix, p. 115

2   Patrick Maume, *Introduction to the Philosophy of Irish Ireland*, p.
     xi

3   Patrick Maume, *Life That is Exile*, p. 9

4   Patrick Maume, *D.P. Moran*, p. 3

5   Brian Inglis, 'Moran of *The Leader*' in *The Shaping of Modern
     Ireland*, p. 110

6   *The Leader,* Golden Jubilee 1950, 21 October, Vol. LCVIII, No. 21, p. 7

7   Peter Kavanagh, *Patrick Kavanagh: A Life Chronicle,* p. 260

8   Brian Inglis, *West Briton,* p. 169

9   *Ibid.,* p. 171

10   Peter Kavanagh, *Lapped Furrows,* p. 171

11   Peter Kavanagh, *The Dancing Flame,* Preface, p. v

12   Brendan Lynch, *Parsons Bookshop,* p. 40

13   *Ibid.,* pp. 47–48

14   Peter Kavanagh, *Lapped Furrows,* p. 171

15   Peter Kavanagh, *The Dancing Flame,* Preface, p. v

16   Kavanagh Collection, UCD Kav/B/68 (5a)

17   Kavanagh Collection, UCD Kav/B/68 (7)

18   Peter Kavanagh, *Lapped Furrows,* p. 172

19   *Ibid.*

Chapter 11

1   Peter Kavanagh, *Patrick Kavanagh: A Life Chronicle,* p. 262

2   *Ibid.*

3   *Irish Press,* 3 February 1954, p. 4

4   Anthony J. Jordan, *John A. Costello 1891–1976: Compromise Taoiseach,* p. 17

5   Jack White, 'The Kavanagh Case', *Spectator,* 5 March 1954, p. 256

6   Anthony Cronin, *Dead as Doornails,* p. 102

7   Michael McInerney, quoted in *John A. Costello*

8   *Irish Times,* 'Irishman's Diary', 9 February 1954, p. 5

9   Kavanagh Collection, UCD Kav/B/69 b

10   *Irish Times,* 4 February 1954, p. 9

11   *Ibid.,* p. 9

12   *Ibid.*

13   *Irish Independent,* 4 February 1954, p. 8

14   Kavanagh Collection, UCD Kav/B/68 (1)

15   *Irish Independent,* 5 February 1954, p. 8

16   *Irish Times,* 5 February 1954, p. 3

17   Marc McDonald, *Irish Law of Defamation,* p. 209

18   *Irish Independent,* 5 February 1954, p. 8

19   *Irish Times,* 5 February 1954, p. 1

20   Patrick Kavanagh, *Collected Pruse,* pp. 172–173

21   *Ibid.,* pp. 173–174

22   *Irish Independent,* 5 February 1954, p. 8

23   Anthony Cronin, *Dead as Doornails,* p. 102

Chapter 12

1   *Irish Times,* 9 February 1954, p. 3

2   Alan Reeve, actually a New Zealander

Chapter 13

1   *Evening Herald,* 9 February 1954, p. 1

2   *Irish Times,* 'Irishman's Diary', 9 February 1954, p. 5

3   Costello papers, UCD Archives P190/610 (33)

4   John Ryan, *Remembering How We Stood,* p. 113

5   *Ibid.,* p. 113

6   Ulick O'Connor, *Brendan Behan,* p. 164

7   Anthony Cronin, *Dead as Doornails,* p. 103

8   Costello papers, UCD Archives P190/605 (43)

Chapter 14

1   John Ryan, *Remembering How We Stood,* pp. 112–113

2   *Evening Herald,* 10 February 1954, p. 3

3   Ulick O'Connor, *Brendan Behan,* p. 164

4   Peter Kavanagh, *Patrick Kavanagh: A Life Chronicle,* p. 265

5   *Ibid.,* pp. 250–251

Chapter 15

1   John Ryan, *Remembering How We Stood,* p. 113

Chapter 16

1   Peter Kavanagh, *Lapped Furrows,* p. 173

2   Peter Kavanagh, *Patrick Kavanagh: A Life Chronicle,* p. 265

3   *Irish Press,* 13 February 1954, p. 1

4   Brendan Lynch, *Parsons Bookshop,* p. 129

5   Peter Kavanagh, *Patrick Kavanagh: A Life Chronicle*, p. 268
6   Peter Kavanagh, *Lapped Furrows*, pp. 173–174
7   Peter Kavanagh, *Lapped Furrows*, p. 145
8   Anthony Cronin, *Dead as Doornails*, p. 101
9   *Ibid.*, pp. 123–124

Chapter 17

1   John Ryan, *Remembering How We Stood*, p. 113
2   *Ibid.*
3   Kavanagh Collection, UCD Kav/B/68 (10)
4   *Ibid.* (11)
5   *Ibid.* (9)
6   Jack White, 'The Kavanagh Case', *Spectator*, 5 March 1954, p. 256
7   Kavanagh Collection, UCD Kav/B/70 (30)
8   *Ibid.* (31)
9   *Ibid.* (28)
10   Peter Kavanagh, *Lapped Furrows*, p. 176
11   Kavanagh Collection, UCD Kav/B/70 (10)
12   *Ibid.* (35)
13   *Ibid.* (34)
14   *Ibid.* (46)
15   *Irish Times*, 18 February 1954, p. 4
16   *Irish Independent*, 10 March 1954, p. 4
17   Peter Kavanagh, *Lapped Furrows*, p. 175
18   Peter Kavanagh, *Patrick Kavanagh: A Life Chronicle*, p. 272
19   Kavanagh Collection, UCD Kav/B/68 (12)
20   *Ibid.* (15)
21   *Ibid.* (16)
22   *Ibid.*, UCD Kav/B/70 (14)

Chapter 18

1   Peter Kavanagh, *Beyond Affection*, p. 152
2   *Irish Times*, 18 November 1954, p. 9
3   *Ibid.*, 19 November 1954, p. 3
4   Peter Kavanagh, *Beyond Affection*, p. 153

5   Kavanagh Collection, UCD Kav/B/83 (46)

6   Peter Kavanagh, *Patrick Kavanagh: A Life Chronicle,* p. 273

7   Peter Kavanagh, *Lapped Furrows,* p. 185

8   *Ibid.,* p. 186

9   Kavanagh Collection, UCD Kav/B/83 (61)

10   Peter Kavanagh, *Lapped Furrows,* p. 186

11   *Ibid.,* p. 187

12   Peter Kavanagh, *Patrick Kavanagh: A Life Chronicle,* p. 277

13   Brendan Lynch, *Parsons Bookshop,* p. 41

14   *Ibid.,* p. 66

15   Antoinette Quinn, *Patrick Kavanagh: A Biography,* p. 341

16   Peter Kavanagh, *Beyond Affection,* p. 156

17   Peter Kavanagh, *Patrick Kavanagh: A Life Chronicle,* p. 68

18   Peter Kavanagh, *Sacred Keeper,* p. 282

19   Peter Kavanagh, *Beyond Affection,* p. 159

20   Peter Kavanagh, *Patrick Kavanagh: A Life Chronicle,* pp. 263–264

21   Kavanagh Collection, UCD Kav/E/1

22   Peter Kavanagh, *Patrick Kavanagh: A Life Chronicle,* p. 281

23   Costello papers, UCD Archives P190/825 (7)

24   Peter Kavanagh, *Patrick Kavanagh: A Life Chronicle,* p. 281

25   *Ibid.,* p. 286

26   Self-portrait RTÉ, first broadcast 30 October 1962

27   Nimbus 1956 in *November Haggard,* p. 45

28   Peter Kavanagh, *Patrick Kavanagh: A Life Chronicle,* appendix 3, p. 420

29   Marc McDonald, *Irish Law of Defamation,* p. 247

30   *Irish Independent,* 15 April 1955, p. 3

31   Peter Kavanagh, *Lapped Furrows,* p. 179

32   *Ibid.,* p. 189

33   Antoinette Quinn, *Patrick Kavanagh: A Biography,* p. 345

34   Costello papers, UCD Archives P190/828 (12)

35   *Ibid.*

36   Antoinette Quinn, *Patrick Kavanagh: Born-again Romantic,* p. 338

37   Antoinette Quinn, *Patrick Kavanagh: A Biography,* p. 316

38   Kavanagh Collection, UCD Kav/B/68 (1)

39   Peter Kavanagh, *Patrick Kavanagh A Life Chronicle,* p. 266

40   Quoted in Brendan Lynch, *Parsons Bookshop,* pp. 39–40

41   Patrick Kavanagh, *Almost Everything,* Track 1

42   Kavanagh Collection, UCD Kav/B/83 (66)

43   *Ibid.*

Bibliography

Bardwell, Leland, *A Restless Life,* Dublin: Liberties Press, 2008

Brown, Terence, *Ireland: A Social and Cultural History,* London: Fontana, 1990

Butler, Hubert, *Escape from the Anthill,* Mullingar: Lilliput, 1985

Cooney, John, *John Charles McQuaid,* Dublin: O'Brien Press, 1999

Cronin, Anthony, *Dead as Doornails,* Dublin: Lilliput Press, 1991

— *No laughing matter,* Dublin: New Island, 2003

Donleavy, J.P., *J.P. Donleavy's Ireland in All of Her Sins and in Some of Her Graces,* London: Michael Joseph, 1986

Gray, Tony, *Mr Smyllie, Sir,* Dublin: Gill & Macmillan, 1991

Greacen, Robert, *Brief Encounters,* Dublin: Cathair Books, 1991

— *Even Without Irene,* Dublin: Dolmen Press, 1969

— *The Sash my Father Wore,* Edinburgh: Mainstream, 1997

Inglis, Brian, *West Briton,* London: Faber, 1962

Jordan, Anthony J., *John A. Costello 1891–1976: Compromise Taoiseach,* Dublin: Westport Books, 2007

Kavanagh, Patrick, *Almost Everything,* Dublin: Claddagh Records, 1963

— *Collected poems,* London: Penguin, 2005

— *Collected Pruse,* London: Martin, Brian & O'Keefe, 1971

— *The Green Fool,* London: Martin, Brian & O'Keefe, 1971

Kavanagh, Peter, (ed.), *Lapped Furrows,* New York: Peter Kavanagh Hand Press, 1969

— (ed.), *November Haggard,* New York: Peter Kavanagh Hand Press, 1971

— *Beyond Affection,* New York: Peter Kavanagh Hand Press, 1977

— *Sacred Keeper,* Curragh: Goldsmith Press, 1980

— *The Dancing Flame,* New York: Peter Kavanagh Hand Press, 1981

— *Patrick Kavanagh: Man and poet,* Newbridge: Goldsmith Press, 1987

— *Patrick Kavanagh: A Life Chronicle,* New York: Peter Kavanagh Hand Press, 2000

Kavanagh's Weekly (facsimile edition), Newbridge: Goldsmith Press, 1981

Kiely, Benedict, *All the Way to Bantry Bay,* London: Gollancz, 1978

Lynch, Brendan, *Parsons Bookshop,* Dublin: Liffey Press, 2006

Lyons, J.B., *Oliver St. John Gogarty,* Dublin: Blackwater, 1980

Maume, Patrick, *D.P. Moran,* Dublin: Historical Association of Ireland, 1995

— *Life that is Exile : Daniel Corkery and the search for Irish Ireland,* Belfast: Institute of Irish Studies, 1993

McDonald, Marc, *Irish Law of Defamation,* Dublin: Round Hall, 1989

Moran, D.P., *The Philosophy of Irish Ireland,* Dublin: UCD Press, 2006

Nemo, John, *Patrick Kavanagh,* London: George Prior, 1979

Ó Broin, Leon, *Just Like Yesterday,* Dublin: Gill & Macmillan, 1986

O'Brien, C.C. (ed.), *The Shaping of Modern Ireland,* London: Routledge, Kegan, Paul, 1960

O'Connor, Ulick, *Brendan Behan,* London: Hamish Hamilton, 1970

O'Mara, Veronica (ed.), *PS … Of Course,* Dublin: Gandon, 1993

Quinn, Antoinette, *Patrick Kavanagh: A Biography*, Dublin: Gill & Macmillan, 2001

— *Patrick Kavanagh: Born-again Romantic*, Dublin: Gill & Macmillan, 1991

Ryan, John, *Remembering How We Stood*, Dublin: Lilliput Press, 2008

Tracy, Honor, *Mind you, I've Said Nothing! Forays in the Irish Republic*, London: White Lion Publishers, 1973

Warner, Alan, *Clay is the Word*, Dublin: Dolmen Press, 1973

Index

Eason's 81, 85, 92, 203
Eliot, T.S. 244
Envoy, the 18, 36, 37, 46, 63, 64,
　65, 75, 76, 118, 126, 127, 129,
　131, 135, 139, 142, 143, 151,
　159, 163, 166, 168, 171, 193,
　268
Esmonde, John 90, 92, 95, 96,
　97, 99, 101, 102, 109, 118,
　123, 125, 166, 235, 250, 251

F

Farren, Robert 66, 134
Fitzgerald, William O'Brien 95,
　167, 172, 200, 201, 202, 203,
　204, 206, 208, 210, 218, 229,
　230, 235, 236
Furlong, Rory 212

G

Ginnell, Eamon 244
Gogarty, Oliver St John 27, 28,
　29, 44
Greacen, Robert 18, 19, 20, 32,
　73, 112

H

Higgins, Fred R. 62, 63, 132,
　133, 134, 156
Hone, Joseph 244

I

Inglis, Brian 29, 44, 67, 87, 89,
　90, 91
Iremonger, Valentin 267, 268,
　269
Irish Press, the 21, 26, 35, 36,
　225, 237

Irish Times, The 11, 17, 35, 36, 43,
　44, 45, 46, 66, 78, 79, 89, 97,
　104, 118, 136, 137, 141, 147,
　149, 177, 178, 192, 193, 209,
　242, 243, 244, 246, 251

K

Kavanagh's Weekly 9, 10, 11, 50,
　76, 77, 80, 81, 82, 83, 84, 85,
　86, 90, 91, 92, 98, 99, 103,
　149, 152, 153, 171, 172, 173,
　176, 177, 179, 182, 186, 187,
　188, 189, 190, 194, 195, 197,
　209, 213, 216, 227, 246, 251,
　268
Kiely, Benedict 19, 22, 24, 52,
　71, 91

L

Lavery, Cecil 250, 263
Leader, The 9, 12, 29, 87, 88, 89,
　90, 91, 95, 98, 99, 100, 101,
　110, 111, 114, 129, 132, 142,
　150, 151, 159, 160, 163, 166,
　171, 185, 195, 197, 198, 199,
　200, 203, 204, 205, 209, 218,
　219, 221, 222, 230, 235, 236,
　242, 245, 263, 265, 266, 267,
　268

M

MacMahon, James 95, 218, 219,
　220, 221, 222, 223, 224, 235
Maguire, Conor 250, 252, 263
Maguire, Martin 250, 263
Manifold, Deirdre 259, 260
McDaid's 46, 47, 142, 143, 155,
　181, 237